GILL
MELLER

time

A YEAR & A DAY IN THE KITCHEN

photography by Andrew Montgomery

time | What do you think of when you think of time?

Time is yesterday. Time is tomorrow. Time is the split second that you own, right now. Now it's gone.

quadrille

contents

In memory of my mum | 1948-2017

time

What do you think of when you think of time?

Time is yesterday. Time is tomorrow. Time is the split second that you own, right now. Now it's gone.

We hold time like a child, as memories. The memory of a close friend, the touch of your mother's hand holding yours, the pencil lines on the kitchen wall showing how you grew. Time is learning to ride a bike and it's the feeling you remember when you fall off.

It's the next harvest and the storm coming. It's your dreams, your opportunities, your children. It's wishing it never happens and hoping one day it will. It is regret, and in the same breath, forgiveness.

We rise and sleep with the patterns of time, everyone on this Earth is bound up in its cycle. We build our days around the light from the sun; its arc through the sky is our most ancient timepiece. Light has sculpted the arrangements of daily life since the very beginning. Our routines have been moulded by it and our world shaped by it.

Time is made up of circles. As the planet turns we scratch marks on a calendar. These marks give us our months, as well as our four seasons: spring, summer, autumn and winter. Our months and our seasons make up our years.

We spend these years together with our families and our friends in our homes, where we build a world around us we can call our own. Our home is our centre, our core. It's the bridge from where we run things; it's where we pilot our days and ride out our nights.

I can remember all the houses I lived in as a child. I have snapshots in my mind of everything from the light in the morning to the people in the kitchen. These houses often find their way into my dreams at night, beckoning me back into certain rooms, so I never forget their details.

In my earliest years we lived in a beautiful house in a small village in Dorset. It was called The Old Parsonage and had a thatched roof and flagstone floors. The simple conservatory on the east gable was filled with a winding grapevine that would fruit in the summer. The kitchen was cool and bright with windows looking south towards the church and north towards the garden. When my mum washed up or prepared vegetables, she looked out over the beech tree with the swing we all loved, the garden and the vegetable patch. On one side of the kitchen was an old oil-fired Aga and on the other, a pine dresser that my uncle had made. In the middle of the room was a big wooden kitchen table. It was my mum and dad's first home together but, more importantly for me, it was their first kitchen together, and it was in the kitchen that nearly everything of meaning seemed to happen.

We were just babies in that kitchen. It's where we met our mum and her mum. It's where we sat in our high chairs and saw her cooking throughout the day. We learned to eat around that table, we cried at that table, fought at it, slept at it, woke at it, and we learned to laugh together around it. It was at that kitchen table that plans were made for passages, and courses were plotted. It was the table where poems and plays were written and where people would quietly read, talk or listen. It's where they all poured wine, smoked, and sang a thousand songs. It's where we painted pictures, spilled our drinks and ate Mum's spaghetti.

One of my earliest memories is of my dad picking freshly cooked crab at the kitchen table. He laid out sheets of newspaper first, and then used a smart-looking hammer with a stainless-steel top and light wooden handle to crack the shells of the crabs so that he could carefully remove the meat from inside. He worked through the claws first, which I found captivating, and then he would turn his attention to the main body, where the brown meat could be found. I now know, those big crabs were probably the same age as my dad.

During those early years we moved house several times, but in each successive home I remember the kitchen with the same affection as the first.

Our table and dresser always fell into place, bringing the room alive. The kitchen remained our sitting room, office, playroom, library and dining room all in one.

As I grew up in those kitchens, I gradually became immersed in food and cooking. I learned about the power of English mustard, and that lighters explode if you leave them by a cooker. I learned that Opinel knives are really, really sharp and how to swear quite well. My dad taught me that bacon and garlic belong together; my mum taught me how to eat mussels that had been cooked with shallots, white wine and flat-leaf parsley, and that perfectly scrambled eggs on toast can make almost anyone feel better. I learned to love the family salad dressing recipe as well as creamed spinach or anything in a well-made white sauce. I discovered that it was salt and pepper that made my parents' supper taste so much better than ours, and my brother discovered, while standing on the table, that wearing Superman pants and a cape doesn't actually mean you can fly.

One house we lived in was next to an old sheep farm; we spent summers building dens in the hay barn, and then smashing them up. We would explore new ways to use nettles as weapons and plot how to lasso sheep so they could pull us along on our bikes. The kitchen had a big larder, with wooden shelves stacked with jars of fruit jam, pickles, cereals, and tins. There were paper sacks of muddy potatoes and firm white onions on the cool floor. I must have stood in there for hours thinking about what I could eat. My dad dug over an area of the garden for his vegetable patch; he would bring in leeks, runner beans, lettuce and rose-coloured raspberries he picked from the unnetted fruit cage. At the weekends the house was usually full, and the kitchen sang with life and cooking. We had great big fry-ups in the morning or Mum's home-grown tomatoes, simply roasted with salt and marjoram and served on toast. Occasionally we'd have a kedgeree, made with delicate haddock from the local smokery, soft-boiled eggs and fresh coriander, Then, of course, lunch, which could easily lead into supper.

On Sundays there was roast leg of lamb with peas and mint, and potatoes cooked in fat, a little garlic and rosemary.

When my mum went back to work, my dad had to learn how to make simple suppers that he could prepare for us after school. Some became legendary; some, not so much, but his cooking came from the heart. Dad's leek and potato soup, for example, was a winter staple (there's a version of it on page 176). And his liver and bacon with sage and his buttery mash were quite literally the best.

His legacy, however – and his own creation – will be spaghetti with bacon, garlic, Parmesan, olive oil and black pepper (see page 253). He began by sizzling streaky bacon in a large frying pan with plenty of garlic. Once the spaghetti was cooked, it went into the frying pan, too. Then, he added the grated Parmesan by the handful and (here's the secret) he would fry the Parmesan with the spaghetti until it began to crisp on the base of the pan. Then, he'd use a wooden spatula to scrape and scratch at the crunchy and, in some areas, chewy cheese, and that's when the freshly ground black pepper would go in.

From one house to the next, the kitchen remained the centre of our home. It's where the strange lodger was occasionally spotted. It's where the dog died. It's where the incident with the bow and arrow took place. It's where I danced with my mum. It's where I first heard my parents argue and where I saw my dad cry.

As I got older the family dynamic changed. My sister and I would always have friends over, people were constantly passing through our kitchen. It was a meeting place, as much as a place to eat. I remember a kitchen that was open all hours. It's where I'd borrow wine from, occasionally. It's where, one wintry night, I devised my smoked ham, Cheddar and red onion toasties. I fried them in a ridged griddle pan until the buttered, crusty white bread was charred and the cheese was molten – a thing dreams were made of. Our kitchen was a brilliant, inspiring place and full of warmth and love, but everything changed here. I suppose we all grew up here.

We never really know how our time will play out or what will happen tomorrow. In the end, that's what's so wonderful about life.

In 1998 I met Alice. I was in my second year of college and we were studying on the same course. We fell in love in the summer and, by the next, our daughter Isla was born.

Suddenly we had our own little home and a baby. Home was a second-floor flat, with a cupboard-sized kitchen. We had a tiny Baby Belling cooker in the corner that my dad gave us, and a small drop-leaf table given to us by one of Alice's relatives. We didn't have much, but what we did have was ours, and it felt good. Time had come full circle, and although things seemed so different from the life Mum and Dad began, in a funny way they were really just the same. We had a kitchen, we had a table and we had time.

about time

Making time to cook has become one of the most important things I do in my life. When we stop for a moment and do it, even in the simplest sense, it makes us feel good inside. Not only does it nourish our bodies and sustain our minds, but it's vital for our happiness and wellbeing. Cooking has opened my eyes to change. I feel closer to my past, but equally I feel closer to the present and to the environment in which I live, because the things I love to cook and eat are so intrinsically connected to my surroundings. It has enabled me to see how one season turns so gracefully into another. It has inspired the way I think about food every day, and it inspired me to write my first cookbook, *Gather*.

Cooking can be a brilliant way to establish gentler, healthier rhythms in the way we live, as families and as individuals. It is a way to mark the passing of time; it is a way to celebrate it, but also remember it. I believe that every time we make something good to eat, we make a memory.

There are recipes in this book that I've been cooking for many years. When I sit down and eat the dishes, they take me back to an exact point in my life. Back to the kitchen of our little townhouse or back to a particular night's work at River Cottage. They can remind me of conversations I've had, and things that, over time, I've learned. People say that when it comes to recipes, everything's been done before – that there is no such thing as a new recipe and, if a dish is different, it's just a spin on something from the past. That could be true, but there are recipes in this book that are new to me. They are ideas and combinations that, up until now, I haven't thought of or heard of before.

On the whole, my new recipes are inspired by the seasonal ingredients I have to hand, and by a love of simple cooking. But I'm sure there's something else involved, too; something special that inspires me. The alchemy of memory, perhaps? A moment in time, I've kept somewhere in my mind? The fragrance of melting sugar at a funfair, wasps in a plum orchard, catching shrimps in Cornwall, even something I read or overheard once. Perhaps I'll never know quite what. There are recipes here that have personal meaning to me – something my mum made, or one of the dishes I cooked in my first home with my young family. These are recipes I want to preserve, but also share. And not just at my kitchen table with my lot, but with you at yours. Among all this, there are recipes that I simply enjoy cooking; recipes that make me feel at home. Many of these will be as familiar to you as they are to me. Roast pork with apples, for example, or homemade baked beans – as timeless as they are delicious.

I've divided this book up into three chapters. Each represents a different time of day – morning, day and night, the moments we nearly always find ourselves in the kitchen. Each chapter flows gently through a year too, marking it in the way I love, with simple seasonal recipes and delicious things to eat. This book is an ode to the kitchen and all it represents. It's a thank you to the kitchens of my childhood, but it's also a letter to the people I've met in them and a menu of the things I've cooked. It's a portrait of a year through the lens of a day. It is a dedication to, and celebration of, time.

these kitchens

No two kitchens are the same; they're all different, yet they all serve the same purpose. Just like our hands – some are soft, others rough, but they can all hold things, they can all make a fist.

It's the brilliant diversity of this space that fascinates me. A kitchen can be both utilitarian and beautiful – or either, individually. A kitchen can be old and haunted with the noise of life, or new and quiet with a knife-sharp clarity.

Gentle, loud, obvious, subtle – kitchens are, in many cases, a reflection of ourselves, who we are and where we are on our journey through life.

A kitchen is like a narration, everything's a clue. Moments are written in splatters on the walls or cuts in the table, and by every pinned postcard or peculiar spoon. Each hook is a home for something from somewhere, every cupboard holds a volume of reference and every shelf reads like a treatise of memories.

As people, we love seeing someone else's world, we're always looking for a way to take a part of it away. We buy magazines to do it, we watch TV shows, and follow hundreds of accounts. But sometimes, we simply stand on the street, and look in through windows, at kitchens.

I'm sure we've all done it, at some point; it's almost impossible not to.

It's in that fleeting, tiptoed moment that we breathe in the scene in real time. We take in the tones from the light, we detect motion, pans or kettles simmering, arms rising and falling. We note colour, the table, books, things on shelves, the clock and the cat.

But what is this? What are we taking away from these kitchens? What are we borrowing? Security, perhaps – there is feeling of security that emanates from a kitchen, like the light from a boat at sea in the night.

A kitchen is the lifeblood of the house and, like the womb, it's where we feed and grow, and where we feel, or have felt safe in the past. The kitchens in this book belong to my family and to my friends. For the most part they represent practical places to cook and to eat. But, beyond that, I feel they go some way towards illustrating the ideas I've set out for you, and both memorialize the time that has passed within them, as well as celebrate the beautiful idiosyncrasies of the families they belong to.

They are windows into worlds.

6.30 A.M. | JUNE

My kitchen
The Summerhouse

MORNING

When she didn't wake up
I knew it wasn't spring
So I fell back into linen and felt your temper outside

Now you meet only to say goodbye
To say you give in
With the voice of a weak creature

My eyes are opened by garden light
And two types of promise
One in the bud, one in the lung

Most things are still the way you left them
Although I've been trying
I still can't tell which bird sings which song

kedgeree

There are some things we eat in our lives that leave a mark on us, a remembrance scar. Some of these things might have been terrible, and the mark is one of distaste. But the majority are, I'd like to think, pleasurable. Kedgeree is one of those dishes for me. I love how unlikely it is: oaky smoked haddock, spices, rice, boiled eggs. Whether its origins lie in Scotland or India, I'm not sure, but it's genius and something I love to make for breakfast or brunch if we have people to stay.

SERVES 4

4 eggs, at room temperature

400ml (14fl oz) whole milk

4 bay leaves

500g (1lb 2oz) undyed smoked haddock or smoked pollack fillets

1 tablespoon extra-virgin olive oil

good knob of butter

2 onions, finely sliced from tip to root

2 teaspoons coriander seeds, crushed

2 teaspoons cumin seeds, crushed

2 teaspoons turmeric

1 teaspoon fenugreek seeds, crushed

4 cardamom pods, bashed

pinch of dried chilli flakes

200g (7oz) basmati rice

1 tablespoon chopped parsley

2 tablespoons chopped coriander, plus whole coriander sprigs, to serve

thinly sliced red chilli, to serve (optional)

1 lemon, cut into wedges

natural yoghurt, to serve

salt and ground black pepper

Bring a medium pan of water to the boil, add the eggs and cook for 6 minutes, which should give you a soft-set yolk. Drain the eggs and run them under the cold tap until cool enough to handle. Carefully shell the eggs and set aside.

Put 400ml (14fl oz) of water into a large pan, then stir in the milk and bay leaves. Set the pan over a medium–high heat. Add the fish fillets (you might need to cut them to fit snugly) and bring the liquid up to a gentle simmer. Cook the fish for 2–3 minutes, then using a slotted spoon or spatula lift the fish carefully out of the pan onto a plate. Turn off the heat and reserve the poaching liquid.

Place another large pan over a medium heat. Add the olive oil and butter and, when bubbling nicely, add the sliced onions. Season the onions with salt and pepper and fry, stirring regularly, for 12–15 minutes, or until the onions are soft and golden. Remove half the onions from the pan and set aside. Add the spices and rice to the remaining onions, stir and cook for a further 1–2 minutes. Pour in the fish poaching liquid, bring to the boil, then reduce the heat and simmer for 8–10 minutes, until the rice is nearly cooked.

While the rice is cooking, discard the fish skin and bones and break the flesh into large flakes. When the rice is nearly cooked, add the fish. Carefully turn the chopped parsley and coriander through the rice and fish mixture. Serve the kedgeree straight from the pan or transfer it to a large serving platter. Halve the boiled eggs and arrange them on top of the kedgeree. Scatter over the remaining fried onions and, if you like, a little thinly sliced fresh red chilli. Serve immediately with lemon wedges, yoghurt and a sprig of coriander.

nettle omelette

My dad always said that the secret to a good omelette is to pour most of the hot, melted butter from the pan into the whisked eggs before you start cooking them. So this is what I do, and it does indeed make a better omelette. Although you could fill this omelette with grated Cheddar cheese or some fried mushrooms, I like this version, with stinging nettles. The nettles are lovely and tender, bright and full of flavour at this time of the year. Take only the top four or six leaves from each plant. You'll need some gloves for picking and washing them, but their sting disappears as soon as you drop them into the hot water.

MAKES 1

1 bowl of nettle tops

2 large eggs

20g (¾oz) butter

salt and freshly ground black pepper

Bring a small pan of salted water to the boil. Add the nettle tops, stirring them into the water with a spoon or fork. Simmer the nettles for 1–2 minutes or until they are tender.

Drain the nettles through a colander, using the back of a spoon to squeeze out any excess liquid. However, don't over-squeeze or the nettles will be too dry. Set aside and keep warm.

Crack the eggs into a medium bowl and whisk together.

Set a small–medium non-stick frying pan over a medium–high heat. Add two-thirds of the butter to the pan and when it's bubbling away pour it into the bowl of whisked eggs. Stir to combine.

Return the pan to the heat and when it's really hot, pour in the buttery eggs. Move them around the pan tipping and tilting and agitating the eggs with the end of a wooden spoon. After 30–40 seconds allow the eggs to settle and cook for a further 30 seconds, until just set. Season the top of the omelette with salt and pepper, then arrange the nettles over one half of the omelette's surface, then dot with the remaining butter. Ease a spatula under the uncovered side of the omelette and fold it gently over. Slide the omelette out onto a warm plate and eat straight away.

potato & wild garlic flat breads with fried eggs & olive oil

These potato flat breads are soft, tender and full of character, and make a somewhat unconventional alternative to toast in the morning. You can flavour them in all sorts of tasty ways, but in the spring I like to use wild garlic. It's a strong and heady herb, but mellows once you've incorporated it into the dough. Later on, in the summer, parsley makes a lovely substitute and works magically with the potatoes and eggs.

MAKES 8

about 200g (7oz) potatoes, peeled and cut into chunks

400g (14oz) strong white bread flour, plus extra for kneading

1 large bunch of wild garlic leaves, finely chopped

2 teaspoons instant dried yeast

1 teaspoon fine salt

TO SERVE

1 knob of butter

4 chicken or duck eggs

4 tablespoons extra-virgin olive oil

wild garlic leaves and flowers, if available (chive flowers also work well)

salt and freshly ground black pepper

Bring the potatoes to the boil in a large pan of salted water. Cook for 15–25 minutes, until tender. Drain in a colander, then leave for 15 minutes to allow the steam to evaporate. Mash until smooth.

Combine the flour, mashed potato, chopped wild garlic leaves, yeast and salt in a large bowl, then gradually stir in up to 250ml (9fl oz) of water, until the mixture forms a soft dough. Turn the dough out onto a lightly floured surface and knead for about 5 minutes, until it feels smooth and elastic, sprinkling on a little more flour only if the dough feels very sticky. Cover and set it aside somewhere warm to double in size. This should take 2–3 hours.

When you're ready, divide the dough equally into eight pieces. Flour your hands and roll each piece into a ball. You can either use a rolling pin to roll out little rounds or simply flatten the balls with your hands. Use plenty of flour, as the dough will be soft and sticky.

Heat a large frying pan over a high heat until hot. Shake off any excess flour from one flat bread and lay it in the hot pan. After a minute or so, check the underside – if you can see dark brown patches, flip it over. Cook the second side for 30–45 seconds, then remove and set aside to keep warm. Repeat for all the flat breads.

To serve, heat another large frying pan over a medium–high heat. Add the butter and, when bubbling, crack in the eggs and fry them to your liking. I prefer them easy-over, so I flip them for a moment.

Top the warm flat breads with the fried eggs. Trickle over the olive oil and season with salt and pepper. If I'm able to get hold of any wild garlic or chive flowers, I like to scatter these over at the last moment.

VEGETARIAN

8.15 A.M. | APRIL

Cameron & Janet's
piano and arrows
Fore Street

buckwheat & oat granola

Granola is easy to make, packed full of healthy, nutritious things and really, really tasty. I have it for breakfast a few times a week, and I know when I have, because I feel better for it. It's good with milk, natural yoghurt or orange juice, or just a few slices of fresh fruit. As with so many things, though, you don't have to reserve this granola for breakfast. It's wonderful scattered over baked apples (page 264) or spooned over vanilla ice cream, too.

MAKES 1 LARGE JAR

300g (10½oz) jumbo oats

75g (2½oz) buckwheat groats

100g (3½oz) mixed nuts, roughly chopped

30g (1oz) pumpkin seeds

30g (1oz) sunflower seeds

good pinch of salt

50ml (1¾fl oz) cold-pressed rapeseed oil

150ml (5fl oz) runny honey

1 egg white

125g (4½oz) chopped dried prunes, dates and raisins

Heat the oven to 150°C/300°F/gas mark 3.

Line your largest baking tray or two smaller ones with baking parchment.

Tumble the oats, groats, nuts, both types of seed, and salt together in a large bowl. Pour over the rapeseed oil and trickle over the honey, then mix everything together well. In a separate bowl, whisk the egg white until light and frothy, then turn this through the mixture.

Spread the granola out over the baking sheet nice and evenly. Place in the oven and bake for 30–35 minutes, turning the mixture with a spatula three or four times during baking. When it's golden and fragrant, it's ready to come out of the oven.

Leave the granola to cool in the tray so that it crisps up nicely. Mix in your chosen dried fruit then transfer to an airtight container or jar. It will keep for about 4–6 weeks.

bacon & kidneys with mustard & cream

When it comes to wonderful breakfasts, this is up there with some of my favourites, and it has to be worth making for the sauce alone. Look for really fresh, firm lambs' kidneys (they're better if they haven't been frozen), and fatty smoked bacon, and make haste in the pan. The handful of chopped parsley that goes in at the end may seem frivolous, but actually the parsley is there for the kidneys, and the kidneys for the parsley.

SERVES 2

splash of extra-virgin olive oil

75g (2½oz) smoked bacon lardons

4 fresh lambs' kidneys, halved and cored

½ glass of white wine or cider

2 heaped teaspoons Dijon mustard

200ml (7fl oz) double cream

1 small bunch of flat-leaf parsley, chopped

2 slices of buttered toast, to serve

salt and freshly ground black pepper

Place a medium frying pan over a high heat. Add a splash of oil followed by the bacon lardons. Let the lardons sizzle away until they begin to render a little fat and take on some colour; about 3–4 minutes. Lightly season the kidneys with salt and pepper, then add them to the frying pan. Initially, don't stir them – let them take on some colour, then after 30 seconds turn them over as best you can.

Cook the kidneys for a further 1 minute, then add the white wine or cider and let the liquid bubble away for a minute or so. Stir in the mustard and the cream, then bring the contents of the pan back to a simmer and reduce for 1–2 minutes, or until the sauce is nice and thick. It should coat the kidneys and bacon.

Add the chopped parsley, then remove the pan from the heat. Pile the kidneys onto the buttered toast and bring to the table straight away.

a simple sourdough

Making a loaf of bread is one of the oldest, simplest forms of cookery, and quite often it can be one of the most rewarding. I tend to bake this sourdough on a Saturday or Sunday, or when I'm working at home. Making it won't take much hands-on time, but you do need to be around every so often to tend to the dough.

MAKES 1 LARGE LOAF

500g (1lb 2oz) strong white bread flour

150g (5½oz) very active starter (it should be thick batter consistency; see below)

325ml (11fl oz) tepid water

10g (¼oz) fine sea salt

rye or wholemeal flour, for dusting

1 medium proving basket

1 x 22–25cm (8½–10in) diameter cast-iron pot

FOR THE STARTER

A starter is fermentation of flour and water that produces 'wild' yeasts and bacteria that make your bread rise and give it flavour.

DAY 1 Place 25g (1oz) rye flour with 50ml (1¾fl oz) warm water in a clean bowl. Stir well, cover and leave overnight in a warm place (at around 30°C/86°F).

DAYS 2, 3 AND 4 Every day add 25g (1oz) rye flour and 50ml (1¾fl oz) warm water. After each addition, stir well, cover and put the mixture back in the warm place. (By Day 3 it should show signs of fermentation.)

DAY 5 You should now have 300g (10½oz) or so of active starter to use in baking. Store the mixture in the fridge, but make sure to feed it once or twice, each time adding a further 25g (1oz) rye flour and 50ml (1¾fl oz) warm water, to ensure it's active before using again. Each time you use a quantity of active starter, replace its weight with a mixture of fresh flour and water in a ratio of 1 part flour to 2 parts water, and allow it to ferment for next time.

If you've overlooked your starter for three or four days, you'll need to refresh it a couple of days before baking. Drop a spoonful into a glass of water – if it floats, the starter's ready to use.

Place the flour and starter in a large mixing bowl. Pour in the water and mix the ingredients into a dough (1–2 minutes). Cover with a plastic bag, and leave to prove in a warm place for 1–2 hours.

Sprinkle over the salt, then scrunch it in with your hands. Now you need to stretch the dough to develop its structure. Think of the surface of the dough as a clock face. Wet your hands and take hold of the edge of the dough at 12 o'clock. Stretch it up out of the bowl, then fold it down onto itself. Do the same at 6 o'clock, then 3, and finally 9. Aim to trap a little air with each fold. Cover again and leave to prove somewhere warm for 1 hour. Repeat the stretching, folding, covering and proving three or four more times. After the final proving, turn out the dough onto a floured work surface and leave it to rest. Liberally sprinkle the proving basket with rye or wholemeal flour. Twice fold the dough through the clock face, then pop the dough into the basket, seams uppermost. Sprinkle the surface with more flour, then cover and leave somewhere warm until it has risen by at least two-thirds and feels light and airy – up to 6 hours.

Preheat your oven to 240°C/475°F/gas mark 9. Place your cast-iron pot in the centre of the oven with the lid on and let it heat up for 10–15 minutes. Carefully remove the lid and quickly turn out the dough into the pot. The surface that was face down in the basket will now be uppermost. Slash the bread across its face. Place the lid on the pot and bake for 20 minutes. Remove the lid and turn down the oven to 180°C/350°F/gas mark 6. Bake for a further 25 minutes. Turn the bread out of the pot onto a rack and allow to cool. It will keep well for a couple of days and toast beautifully for several more.

blackcurrant jam

There's a brilliant film called *Hope and Glory* that my brother and I used to watch a lot as kids. It's about the trials of a family living in London during World War II. The film's full of wonderfully funny scenes, as well as those both sensitive and dark. My favourite bit is when the family opens a tin of German jam that the father has brought back to England. I like the way he opens the tin; I like the way the jam looks and the sound of the spoon on his teeth as he demonstrates 'the jam is not poisoned'; and I love the way everyone's suspicions are alleviated when they taste how delicious the jam really is. This is the jam my mum made, and her mum before her. And that's what's so good about jam – time doesn't change it, and it's the same the world over.

MAKES 6–8 JARS

1kg (2lb 4oz) blackcurrants

1.5kg (3lb 5oz) golden granulated sugar

Carefully pick over the fruit, removing the stalks and loose leaves. I don't tend to worry about the papery dried flower at the tip of the currant, unless it's really obvious. Place the currants into a large heavy-based pan or a preserving pan with 500ml (17fl oz) water. Set the pan over a medium heat and bring to a gentle simmer, stirring once or twice. Cook for 15–20 minutes, or until the fruit is soft and the skins tender, but the currants retain a little shape.

Add the sugar to the pan and stir until it has dissolved, about 4–5 minutes. Turn up the heat and bring the jam to a rolling boil, allowing it to boil for 4–6 minutes. Remove the jam from the heat, then stir for a minute or so to help it cool. Now test the jam for setting point. Just spoon a few drops of jam onto a very cold saucer. Once the jam has cooled, push the surface with your finger, if it wrinkles, then it has reached setting point. Alternatively, use a sugar thermometer to check that the jam reaches 105°C (220°F).

Let the jam cool for a while before you jar it up (if it's too hot the fruit may float to the surface). Ladle the jam into warm, sterilized jars (you can sterilize them by running them through your dishwasher on its highest setting), and seal straight away. Store in a cool, dry place.

peaches with sage, smoked bacon & honey

Fruits that are sweet, floral and fleshy are made for bacon, especially smoked bacon. They play so well with the salty cure, and their softness is a textural gift to crisp rind. You could try this recipe with apples, but there is something about peaches for breakfast that makes me feel good. Honey and sage (I could say those two words over and over) are very much natural additions to this, the simplest of recipes.

SERVES 2

½ tablespoon extra-virgin olive oil

4 rashers dry-cured smoked back bacon

2 ripe peaches, halved and stoned

1 handful of sage leaves

1 tablespoon runny honey

salt and freshly ground black pepper

Place a large frying pan over a medium heat. Add the oil, then the bacon rashers. When the rashers are sizzling, add the peaches, cut-side down. After 3–4 minutes turn the fruit and scatter over the sage leaves. Throughout cooking, turn the bacon every so often, until it crisps to your liking.

Divide the peaches and bacon equally between two plates and season the peaches with a little salt and pepper, if they need it. Bring to the table, then trickle with honey immediately before serving.

mushrooms baked on toast with garden herbs, butter & garlic

This all-in-one Autumn breakfast takes minutes to prepare. Everything goes into the one tray and gets popped in the oven to bake – it's completely fuss-less. There's a sort of magic that happens as it cooks, which doesn't happen with conventional mushrooms on toast. Essentially, the bread soaks up everything the mushrooms have to offer, so you end up with this wonderfully crunchy-around-the-edge toast with a soft buttery, garlicky centre. What could be better?

SERVES 5

5 slices of good country bread or sourdough

10 large open-cap mushrooms, such as Portobello

50g (1¾oz) chilled butter

5 or 6 thyme sprigs

1 small bunch of parsley, leaves picked and finely chopped

½ small bunch of chives, finely chopped

5 garlic cloves, skin left on, bashed

2 tablespoons extra-virgin olive oil, plus extra to finish

salt and freshly ground black pepper

Heat the oven to 190°C/375°F/gas mark 6½.

Arrange the slices of bread over a large baking tray. Place the mushrooms on top of the bread; it doesn't matter if they overhang.

Slice the butter thinly and place a few pieces on each mushroom. Scatter the thyme sprigs and chopped herbs over the top of the butter and mushrooms, along with the garlic. Season with plenty of salt and pepper. Finally, trickle with the olive oil.

Place the mushrooms in the oven and bake for 15–20 minutes, or until the mushrooms are collapsed and tender and the toast is crunchy around the edges. Serve at once.

autumn wild mushroom & sausage chachouka

There is a point in this recipe, or in any interpretation of a chachouka for that matter, that I struggle with. It is the point at which you crack raw eggs into a pan of perfectly cooked food. My reaction is momentary and outwardly unnoticeable, but I know it's there. It is a sense of unease or illogic. A fraction of a second later, it is forgotten, and all I see again is the perfection in the pan and the harmony between its contents. Wild mushrooms are certainly not essential here. You can use firm little chestnut mushrooms or large Portobello, or any variety you like.

SERVES 2–3

splash of extra-virgin olive oil

3 sausages

1 knob of butter

1 small onion, thinly sliced

1 handful of wild mushrooms or the equivalent weight in cultivated mushrooms, such as chestnut

handful of sage leaves, roughly chopped

3 or 4 thyme sprigs, leaves picked

1 tablespoon chopped parsley leaves

3 tablespoons crème fraîche

3 eggs

salt and freshly ground black pepper

Heat the grill to hot.

Heat a large ovenproof frying pan over a medium heat and add the splash of oil, followed by the sausages. Cook the sausages gently for 12–15 minutes, turning regularly until all sides are lovely and golden. Take the sausages out of the pan and discard the excess fat.

Return the pan to the heat, add the knob of butter, followed by the sliced onion, the mushrooms, and the sage, thyme and parsley leaves. Season everything with a little salt and black pepper. Fry, stirring regularly, until the onion is starting to caramelize and the mushrooms are just cooked, about 8–10 minutes.

Cut the sausages into thick slices and add to the pan with the mushrooms. Cook for a further 3–4 minutes, until the sausage slices have heated through. Stir in the crème fraîche and bring to a simmer. Allow everything to bubble away for 1–2 minutes to thicken a little. Make three little wells in the pan in between the mushrooms and sausages and carefully crack in the eggs. Cook the eggs gently for 3–4 minutes, until the whites have just begun to set. Then, place the entire pan under the grill for 1 minute or so, just to cook the tops of the eggs. Serve straight away with toast on the side.

smoked haddock & chard toasts

I'm not really sure how to describe this. It's not a rarebit, it's not a croque of any sort either, and it certainly pushes the boundaries of cheese on toast. So I'm thinking of giving it a new genre all of its own, and I'm calling that 'Combine-things-you-love-together-on-toast toasts'. I think it has a certain ring to it. If you can't find chard, then spinach will work in just the same way.

SERVES 2

150g (5½oz) smoked haddock whole milk, for poaching

30g (1oz) butter

20g (¾oz) plain flour

20g (¾oz) mature Cheddar cheese, grated

1 teaspoon Dijon mustard

1 bunch of chard

2 large slices of toasted sourdough

salt and freshly ground black pepper

Heat the grill to high.

Put the smoked haddock into a medium pan, you may need to cut it so that it fits in snugly. Pour over enough milk to just cover. Bring the liquid up to a gentle simmer and cook for 1–2 minutes, until the fish starts to flake easily to indicate it is just cooked, then turn off the heat. Remove the fish using a slotted spoon, and set aside. Reserve the milk. When the haddock is cool enough to handle, break it into large flakes, removing any bones or bits of skin as you go.

Melt the butter in a medium pan over a medium heat until it begins to bubble, then stir in the flour and cook gently for 2–3 minutes to cook out the flour. Gradually add about 150ml (5fl oz) of the reserved poaching milk, stirring all the time as you do so. When the sauce is smooth and thick, let it cook for 1–2 minutes, then add the Cheddar, the mustard and some salt and black pepper to taste. Remove from the heat and keep warm.

Bring a small pan of water to the boil. Add the chard leaves and cook for 2–3 minutes, until tender. Drain well, squeezing out the excess liquid with the back of a spoon, then fold the chard into the sauce along with the flaked fish.

Carefully spread the mixture over the toasted sourdough and place under the hot grill for 3–4 minutes, until bubbling and golden. Serve straight away.

homemade baked beans

These beans aren't quite the same as the ones that come in a can. I'd say they're more life changing. They make a heart-warming breakfast on their own or piled onto warm, buttered toast, but could just as easily be served in the evening alongside some smoky sausages or crispy fried squid. I adore the fragrant herbs, the citrus notes from the coriander seeds and the rich sweetness that comes from molasses.

SERVES 6–8

300g (10½oz) dried haricot
or cannellini beans

2 tablespoons fine salt,
for soaking the beans

2 tablespoons extra-virgin
olive oil

2 onions, halved and thinly sliced

2 garlic cloves, finely chopped

1 teaspoon smoked paprika

1 teaspoon cracked coriander
seeds

4 bay leaves

3 or 4 thyme sprigs

1 rosemary sprig

1 x 400g (14oz) tin good-quality
chopped tomatoes

1 teaspoon Dijon mustard

2 tablespoons soft brown sugar

½ tablespoon molasses

4 tablespoons cider vinegar

salt and freshly ground
black pepper

Place the dried beans in a large bowl and cover with water. Add the fine salt, give the beans a stir and allow them to soak for 10–12 hours or overnight.

Drain the beans and place them in a large pan. Cover with more water and set over a medium–high heat. Bring to a simmer and cook until tender, about 35–40 minutes.

Meanwhile set a large heavy-based casserole over a medium–low heat. Add the olive oil followed by the sliced onions. Season with a little salt and pepper and cook, stirring regularly, for 10–12 minutes, until the onions have softened. Add the garlic, smoked paprika, coriander seeds and all the herbs. Cook for a further 2–3 minutes, then add the canned tomatoes plus half a can of water, and the mustard, sugar, molasses and vinegar and stir well. Bring to a simmer and cook uncovered over a low heat for about 2 hours, until you have a rich, deep-flavoured sauce that will cling to the tender beans. You might need to top up with water if the mixture looks a little dry. Add the beans and cook for a further 15–20 minutes, then remove from the heat and allow the beans to stand for 10 minutes before tasting, adjusting the seasoning, if necessary, and serving.

buckwheat pancakes

These buckwheat pancakes are far more delicious than their equivalent made with white wheat flour. They have an almost crisp surface, but have softness within to give them lots of texture, which pancakes often lack. What's more, they're gluten free. They're wonderful for breakfast with some fruit jam or some lemon and sugar. And they're also great for supper, stuffed with ham, spinach and rich cheese sauce.

MAKES ABOUT 4

100g (3½oz) buckwheat flour

pinch of salt

1 egg

300ml (10½fl oz) milk

50g (1¾oz) butter, melted

Place the flour and salt in a large bowl. Make a well in the centre and crack in the egg. Pour in half the milk and whisk until you have a thick, smooth batter. Pour in the remaining milk and whisk again. You're aiming for the consistency of double cream. Cover the batter and refrigerate until needed.

When you're ready to cook the pancakes, heat a large non-stick frying pan over a low heat. Add the butter and when it's bubbling, pour nearly all of it into the bowl of batter and whisk.

Use a ladle to spoon the pancake batter into the pan, then tilt the pan to spread the mixture out evenly.

As it sets shake the pan to see if the pancake is loose, then flip it over with a palette knife. Cook the other side for 30–40 seconds, until golden, then slide the pancake out onto a warm plate. Repeat until you have used up all the remaining batter.

Serve the pancakes warm with a good lemon curd, blackcurrant jam (see page 32) and yoghurt.

7.40 A.M. | OCTOBER

Julian & Diana's
where the girls grew up
Burrow Hill

spelt waffles with fruit in tea, cardamom & honey

The only thing my youngest daughter really wanted for Christmas was a waffle maker. It turned out she got one. (Nothing to do with me, honest.) Before she leaves for school in the morning, she makes herself some waffles. Once she's gone, I make myself some, too! This is one of my favourite ways to eat them. The plump, tea-soaked fruit is delicious on just about anything, but works best with crisp, light, nutty spelt waffles.

MAKES 4–6

200g (7oz) spelt flour

pinch of fine salt

1 teaspoon baking powder

2 eggs, separated

200ml (7fl oz) whole milk

25g (1oz) soft brown sugar

50g (1¾oz) butter, melted

natural yoghurt, to serve

FOR THE FRUIT IN TEA

200g (7oz) mixed dried fruit, including apricots, figs, prunes and raisins

2 cardamom pods, split

1 vanilla pod, split

1 teaspoon black peppercorns

2 bay leaves

1 thyme sprig (optional)

1 English breakfast tea bag

1 tablespoon runny honey

1 tangerine or clementine, halved

First, make the fruit in tea. Place all the ingredients, except the tangerine or clementine, in a small pan. Then, squeeze in the juice from the tangerine or clementine halves and chuck the halves into the pan as well. Pour over 200ml (7fl oz) of water and place the pan over a medium heat. Bring the liquid up to a simmer, cook for 1 minute, then remove the pan from the heat and transfer the contents to a heatproof bowl. Once cool, discard the tea bag and place the bowl in the fridge. Allow the fruit to plump up for 12 hours or, better still, overnight.

To make the waffles, combine the spelt flour, salt and baking powder in a large bowl.

Put the egg yolks in a medium bowl and whisk together with the milk and sugar and pour this into the flour mixture, whisking as you do so. Keep whisking until you have a smooth, thick batter.

In a separate bowl, whisk the egg whites until they hold a peak, then fold these into the batter. Finally, stir in about half a tablespoon of the melted butter.

Heat your waffle irons until hot, then brush them with the remaining butter. Ladle in some batter and cook until risen and golden.

To serve, place a warm waffle or two on each plate. Top with a spoonful of thick natural yoghurt and finish with a heaped spoonful of fruit in tea.

figs with yoghurt, honey & roasted barley crumble

I know of only one fig tree here in southwest England that produces fruit that actually ripens to perfection. The owner of the tree sends a few kilos down to River Cottage each year, which is such a treat. A fig in the right condition – that being sweet, soft (but not overly) and dark blue and red, like a bloody bruise – is a thing so wonderful you need little else of a morning. This recipe, which I'll call a 'weekend breakfast', has a feeling of the Mediterranean about it: figs, fragrant thyme, thick, sour yoghurt, and honey in the comb.

SERVES 4–6

400ml (14fl oz) thick Greek yoghurt

6 perfectly ripe figs

2–3 tablespoons runny honey and honeycomb

few thyme sprigs (optional)

FOR THE BARLEY CRUMBLE

100g (3½oz) plain flour

pinch of fine salt

100g (3½oz) butter, cubed and chilled

75g (2½oz) golden caster sugar

75g (2½oz) barley flakes

First, make the barley crumble. Heat the oven to 175°C/335°F/gas mark 5½. Combine all the ingredients in a large bowl. Mix and rub the ingredients thoroughly together until you have formed clumps and lumps.

Line a large baking tray with a piece of baking parchment. Tip out the mixture onto the tray and distribute evenly. Place in the oven for 20–30 minutes, turning the crumble over three or four times during baking, until it is evenly golden all over. Remove from the oven.

To construct the dish, spoon the yoghurt out onto a large serving plate or platter and spread it evenly over the base. Halve the figs, or quarter them if they are large, and scatter the pieces over the yoghurt. Cut the honeycomb up into small sticky bits and distribute this in, around and over the figs.

Scatter over a few generous handfuls of the barley crumble, and finish off with a little shake of leaves from the thyme sprig, if using.

purple sprouting broccoli with smoked paprika, yoghurt & eggs

This is my spin on traditional Turkish eggs and it makes a brilliant breakfast. I love the addition of purple sprouting broccoli, which gives the dish more substance and is perfect for scooping up the smoky, dressed yoghurt and soft poached egg.

SERVES 2

1 tablespoon cider vinegar

2 very fresh eggs

250g (9oz) purple sprouting broccoli

50g (1¾oz) butter

1 garlic clove, thinly sliced

1 rosemary sprig

2 teaspoons sweet smoked paprika

4 tablespoons natural yoghurt

salt and freshly ground black pepper

Bring a medium pan of water to the boil and add the vinegar. Twirl a spoon in the water to make a mini whirlpool. Crack in the eggs, turn the heat down to low and cook for 2½–3 minutes, until the eggs are soft poached. (Remember: the fresher the eggs, the better they poach.) Remove the eggs carefully with a slotted spoon. Set aside to keep warm.

Bring another larger pan of salted water to the boil, add the purple sprouting broccoli and simmer for a couple of minutes. It wants to retain a slight bite to the stem. Drain the broccoli and allow it to steam off for a moment.

Meanwhile, melt the butter in a small pan. When it's bubbling, add the garlic, rosemary and smoked paprika. Cook the garlic for 1 minute or so, until softened but not browned, then remove the pan from the heat.

Divide the natural yoghurt between two warm bowls. Arrange the broccoli in the bowls and place the poached eggs alongside. Season everything with a little salt and pepper and finish by spooning over the hot, smoky butter. Serve at once.

10.15 A.M. | NOVEMBER

Olly & Kerry's
built with his hands for them
Fivepenny Farm

oliver's bloody mary

Sometimes you meet someone and it feels like they've entered your life for a reason; and that the time you spend together will become important later on, in the future. Quite often their approach might change the way you do things and your approach might change their ways, too. Oliver's Bloody Mary changed the way I make this classic. It was such a bold, brilliant cure that it made me smile from the inside out.

SERVES 8–10

1 teaspoon sweet smoked paprika

2–3 teaspoons Tabasco

3 teaspoons Worcestershire sauce

2 teaspoons sherry vinegar

2 teaspoons soft brown sugar

1 teaspoon celery salt, plus extra to serve

½ teaspoon freshly ground black pepper, plus extra to serve

350ml (12fl oz) horseradish vodka (see below), chilled

about 1 litre (35fl oz) good-quality tomato juice, chilled

sticks of leafy, tender celery to go around, and some thyme sprigs, to serve

FOR THE HORSERADISH VODKA

1 horseradish root

2 thyme sprigs

1 tablespoon runny honey

1 litre (35fl oz) good-quality vodka

You can make this Bloody Mary using any good-quality vodka, but I like to use horseradish-infused vodka, which I prepare in advance, anticipating the day I'll need it. To flavour the vodka, peel the horseradish root, then slice it carefully with a very sharp knife into long, thin lengths. Place the horseradish and sprigs of thyme into a clean, 1 litre (35fl oz) glass bottle. In a small bowl combine the honey with a splash of vodka and stir to dissolve. Pour this into the bottle with the horseradish and thyme and top up with the remaining vodka.

Leave the bottle in a dark place for the vodka to infuse for three to five days. When you're ready, pass the vodka through a sieve, discarding the horseradish (or use it to make a sauce) and thyme sprigs. Return the flavoured vodka to the bottle and seal. It'll be good for many months.

To make the Bloody Mary, whisk the smoked paprika, Tabasco, Worcestershire sauce, vinegar, sugar, celery salt and black pepper together in a large, broad jug. Pour over the vodka and tomato juice and stir well.

Divide the Bloody Mary equally between clean glasses, then bless each one with a celery stick, a sprig of thyme, a pinch of celery salt and a twist of black pepper. Serve at once.

brussels tops, chorizo, onions & fried egg

Brussels tops are just as delicious and nutritious as the sprouts themselves, but not everyone knows that. They crown each plant and each plant has only one. During the winter months, seek them out – you'll find them in greengrocers and farm shops from November onwards. They have a little spring to their green and a delicate character, and they fry up perfectly for breakfast.

SERVES 2

1 firm Brussels top

2 tablespoons extra-virgin olive oil

100g (3½oz) chorizo, sliced into 1cm (½in) thick rounds

1 onion, sliced

1 garlic clove, sliced

2 rosemary sprigs

1 small knob of butter

2 eggs

salt and freshly ground black pepper

Bring a large pan of salted water to the boil. Add the whole Brussels top, return to a simmer and cook for 1–2 minutes, until just tender. Drain well.

Heat a large frying pan over a medium heat. Add the olive oil and when hot add the chorizo, the sliced onion and garlic, and the rosemary. Season with a little salt and pepper and cook, stirring regularly, for 8–10 minutes or until the onions are soft and beginning to caramelize.

Spoon the chorizo and onions to one side of the pan. Slice the sprout top exactly in half down its core, season the two halves with salt and pepper, and add them to the pan, cut-side down. Fry the sprout tops for 2–3 minutes on each side until lightly charred.

Divide the chorizo and Brussels tops equally between two warmed plates. Add the butter to the pan and when it's bubbling crack in the eggs and fry gently to your liking. Place the eggs on the plates and spoon over any spicy, fatty butter from the pan. Then, place all this in your face.

bubble & squeak, fried pig's cheek & poached egg

Bubble and squeak was something we used to eat on one of the quieter, slower mornings after Christmas Day. There always seemed to be cooked, cold sprouts left over and maybe some mashed potato (never any roast potatoes, though), which was a fairly typical accompaniment to the Boxing Day ham. Fry mash and sprouts and salty-sweet bacon, or in this case *guanciale*, or cured pig's cheek, and you have a wonderful breakfast. Poached or fried eggs are optional (really meaning mandatory).

SERVES 2

1 knob of butter

1 tablespoon extra-virgin olive oil

1 onion, sliced

about 200g (7oz) cooked sprouts, sliced thinly

250g (9oz) cold mashed potato

2 thick slices cured pig's cheek or pancetta

1 tablespoon cider vinegar

2 eggs

salt and freshly ground black pepper

Heat the oven to low, or turn on the warming oven, if you have one.

To make the bubble-and-squeak mixture, heat a medium non-stick frying pan over a medium heat. Add the butter and olive oil and, when it's bubbling, add the onion. Cook, stirring regularly for 10–12 minutes, until the onion is soft and sweet. Use a slotted spoon to transfer the onion from the pan to a large bowl. Add the sliced sprouts to the onion, along with the cold mashed potato. Season with salt and pepper.

Place the sliced pig's cheek into the hot pan and fry for 2–3 minutes on each side, until lovely and crispy on the outside and soft in the middle. Remove from the pan and keep the cheek warm in the low oven. Turn up the heat under the pan and add the bubble-and-squeak mixture. Fry, flipping, cutting and turning it all as it browns and crisps in the pan.

Meanwhile, bring a medium pan of water to the boil and add the vinegar. Twirl a spoon in the water to make a mini whirlpool. Crack the eggs in, turn the heat down to low and cook for 2½–3 minutes, until the eggs are soft-poached. (Remember: the fresher the eggs, the better they poach.) Remove the eggs carefully with a slotted spoon. Set aside to keep warm.

To serve, place the pig's cheeks onto warmed plates next to a spoonful of bubble and squeak and a poached egg, then crack over some salt and black pepper, if you wish.

11.00 A.M. | NOVEMBER

Tristan Connell
thank you
The beach hut

homemade bacon

This is an incredibly simple way to make your own lovely bacon. Anyone can do it, you don't need any special equipment, nothing can really go wrong and the results are so fantastic that I'd recommend it to anyone who enjoys good food and cooking. You begin by making a dry cure, which is a combination of salt, sugar, spices and herbs. You then apply this to the pork. Five days later you have bacon. I like to hang the whole bacon somewhere cool and dry for several weeks before slicing it, but it will keep for months once cured.

2.5kg (5lb 8oz) piece of pork belly, cut from the thick end, ribs removed

FOR THE DRY CURE

300g (10½oz) fine salt

200g (7oz) soft brown or demerara sugar

2 tablespoons lightly crushed coriander seeds

2 tablespoons cracked black peppercorns

2 or 3 rosemary sprigs, leaves picked and roughly chopped

1 small bunch of thyme, leaves picked

2 garlic cloves, peeled and thinly sliced (optional)

First, make the dry cure. Place all the ingredients, including the herbs and the garlic, if using, in a large bowl and mix well. Scatter a handful of the cure over the bottom of a large plate or tray. This needs to be big enough to take your piece of pork belly, but small enough to fit in the fridge. Lay the pork belly on the cure, then scatter over another handful. Make sure you apply a little cure to all the cut surfaces of the pork. Aim to use about 100g (3½oz) in total. Cover and leave in the fridge for 24 hours. Reserve the remaining cure.

The next day, pour off the liquid that the salt has drawn out of the meat. Apply a second scattering of dry cure in the same way, a little underneath and a little on top, and return to the fridge. Repeat the process for three more days (five days in total).

Rinse any cure residue from the bacon under cold running water, then pat the bacon dry with a clean tea towel. If you make your bacon during the winter, hang it up to dry outside, out of direct sunlight and the rain, and where plenty of cool air can move around it. Under a porch is ideal, or in an airy shed or garage.

As the temperature warms up and the flies come back, it's better to let your bacon air dry in the fridge. Simply leave uncovered on a clean, dry tea towel. I like to air dry my bacon for a few weeks before I begin eating it. During this time it will become firmer and develop flavour. Once the bacon is dry, you can keep it wrapped in a clean tea towel in the fridge for several months.

baked eggs with bacon, cream & thyme

My good friend Simon Wheeler, whom I've worked with for many years, inspired me to start cooking these baked eggs. He told me about something similar he used to be served in a big country house in Ireland when he was a boy. He said that while he was there, the house produced its own bacon, cream, eggs and thyme, but it wouldn't be like that any more. I didn't want just to imagine how good all that tasted, so I made a version myself. It's a simple, quick, rich little breakfast that I like with some buttered malted brown toast.

SERVES 2

4 thin rashers of streaky bacon

2 thyme sprigs

2 marjoram sprigs (optional)

4 tablespoons double cream

2 eggs

salt and freshly ground
black pepper

Heat the oven to 180°C/350°F/gas mark 6.

You'll need two ramekins or similar-sized ovenproof dishes. I like to use quite shallow ones. Place two rashers of streaky bacon into each ramekin along with the thyme sprigs, and the marjoram sprigs, if using. Place the two ramekins on a baking tray, then into the hot oven. Cook for 10–12 minutes, or until the bacon is just beginning to crisp, then remove the tray.

Spoon 2 tablespoons of cream into each ramekin – it will bubble in the bacon fat. Carefully crack an egg into each and return the tray to the oven for a further 8–10 minutes, or until the egg whites are set and the yolks are still runny. Remove from the oven, season with salt and pepper, and serve straight away.

scrambled eggs on marmite toast

I had a wisdom tooth out in my twenties and for some reason the crazy dentist made a real hash of it. I still maintain the experience was equal to, or perhaps more painful than giving birth. The only thing I ate over the following couple of days was my mum's scrambled eggs, made with plenty of butter and salt and pepper. They were always delicious because she cooked them slowly over a low, gentle heat, as if she were making a custard. This is exactly how I make them now. It still surprises people when I say it should take eight to ten minutes to make.

SERVES 2–3

25g (1oz) butter, plus extra for the toast

6 large eggs

2 or 3 slices of good malted or white sourdough

Marmite

salt and freshly ground black pepper

Place a medium non-stick pan over a really low heat. Add the butter and allow it to melt and bubble. Crack the eggs into a measuring jug and whisk them well, then pour them into the bubbling butter. Cook the eggs very, very gently for 8–10 minutes, stirring regularly. I like to use a rubber spatula to do this, but a wooden spoon is fine, too. Good scrambled eggs should look soft and delicate, not firm or rubbery, so take them off the heat before they lose that loose texture.

Toast the bread on both sides and butter generously. Spread the toast with a little Marmite, then spoon the soft scrambled eggs on top. Season to taste and serve straight away.

potato cakes with kimchi & cheddar cheese

Eating something hot and powerful in the morning can help to kick your day into action. It can get the blood pumping around your body and wake up your mouth and mind. Kimchi is a traditional Korean preparation made by salting and fermenting cabbage in a seriously punchy paste made from chilli powder, garlic, ginger and a little fermented shrimp or fish sauce. I love it with something as familiar and simple as a crisp potato cake – the delicate creamy potato within tames the kimchi's lion.

SERVES 2

450g (1lb) floury potatoes, such as Maris Piper or King Edward, peeled and cut into 3–4cm (1¼–1½in) cubes

4 tablespoons extra-virgin olive oil

300g (10½oz) readymade kimchi

75g (2½oz) Cheddar cheese, grated

1 or 2 pinches of sweet paprika

fresh chilli, thinly sliced (optional)

salt and freshly ground black pepper

Bring the potatoes to the boil in a large pan of salted water and cook for 20–30 minutes, or until they are nice and tender. Then, drain them in a colander and leave them there for 15 minutes to allow the steam to evaporate.

Tip the potatoes into a bowl and mash them really well. Season the mash with salt and pepper and form into two firm cakes.

Heat the grill to hot.

Heat the olive oil in a large non-stick ovenproof frying pan over a medium heat. When hot, add the potato cakes and fry for 4–5 minutes on each side, until crisp and golden. Add the kimchi to the pan and turn once or twice to warm through. Scatter over the grated cheese and place the whole pan under the grill for 2–3 minutes, until the cheese is bubbling and popping. Remove the pan and divide the potato cake and kimchi, and all the delicious crisp and soft melted cheese equally between two warm plates. Finish with a pinch of paprika and a few slivers of chilli, if you like an extra dose of heat.

9.20 A.M. | JANUARY

Hugh & Candida's
good bye
Little Place

cold-smoked trout

My wife Alice owns a little shop in our town, and every so often a local fisherman drops off some amazing trout. He charges us only a few pounds for the fish and, more often than not, I'll cure and cold smoke them – they're always delicious.

Cold smoking is much simpler than you may think; anyone can turn their hand to it. I'm lucky because I can use our chimney, which I can reach without worrying about falling to the ground. As the fire below smoulders away gently, a fish hangs quietly near the top, with cool, oak smoke slowly passing it by. In cold smoking, the smoke merely flavours (rather than cooks) the fish, so it shouldn't really go above 25°C (77°F).

In its crudest form a cold smoker is really just a fire chamber and a smoke chamber connected via a pipe long enough to allow the smoke to cool before it reaches the food. At River Cottage we connected an old pot-bellied stove to a cider barrel, but I've heard of people making cold smokers out of wardrobes, gun cupboards, broken fridges and even old-fashioned red phone boxes. You either hang the fish or meat inside or lay it on racks. You can buy small mesh coils that you fill with sawdust or wood chip (hardwoods are best – I like the wood from fruit trees, as well as the wood from the wonderful bay), that you light and place in the bottom of a smoke chamber. They'll smoulder away for many hours.

Always salt and dry your fish before you smoke it. This is important as it firms the surface of the fish and draws outward flavour-carrying particles from inside the flesh. These particles create colour and flavour when exposed to smoke.

300g (10½oz) fine salt

50g (1¾oz) golden granulated sugar

1 large trout (about 2–3kg/ 4lb 8oz–6lb 8oz), filleted and pin boned

Combine the salt and sugar in a bowl. Scatter a quarter of the cure over the base of a large plastic tray. Lay the fish fillets on top, skin-side down and cover with the remaining cure, scattering more cure over the thicker parts of the fish and less over the thinner parts. Leave the fish to salt, uncovered, in the bottom of the fridge for 18–24 hours. Rinse the cure off the fish under a cool running tap. Allow the water to drip off, then pat the fillets dry with kitchen paper or a clean tea towel. Lay the fillets on another clean tea towel, skin-side down and place in the fridge, uncovered for a further 48 hours.

Cold smoke the fish in your newly constructed cold smoker for 10–14 hours, then remove and wrap it in a cloth. Refrigerate for 24 hours before slicing.

parsnip & oat porridge with dates & honey

If you begin your day with oats, you're beginning your day well, because oats are among the healthiest grains you'll ever eat. They're gluten-free whole grains and an important source of fibre and essential vitamins and minerals (including antioxidants). Adding grated parsnip to this recipe can only cement these health benefits, but that's not why it's in there. It's there because I've always liked the combination of oats and parsnips together. They have a natural affinity, whether that's in bread, in salads, in savoury crumbles, or as here, in a porridge for breakfast. Soft, caramelly dates (another good friend to the parsnip) and runny honey turn what is quite a humble meal into a real treat.

SERVES 2

100g (3½oz) large porridge oats

1 parsnip (about 50g/1¾oz), peeled and grated

350ml (12fl oz) whole milk

pinch of salt

8 sticky dates, whole or chopped

runny honey, for trickling

double cream, to serve (optional)

Place the porridge oats and grated parsnip in a medium heavy-based pan (a non-stick one will make the washing up so much easier). Pour over the milk and 350ml (12fl oz) of water, and add the pinch of salt. Set the pan over a medium heat and bring the liquid up to a simmer, stirring regularly. Cook the oats and parsnip mixture for 8–10 minutes, stirring continuously, until it has reached the desired consistency. If it's a little thick, add a splash more water.

Spoon the porridge into wide bowls, top with dates and trickle generously with honey. At the weekend I like to serve it with a dash of cold double cream as well, but perhaps that's just me.

blackcurrant, goat's cheese, hazelnut & rosemary soda bread

This super-quick soda bread is easy to make and incredibly delicious to eat. It's a brilliant way to use a few handfuls of fizzy, sharp blackcurrants, a fruit I've always found perfect alongside goat's cheese, and the perfumed perennial herb rosemary. I think this bread is at its best served warm with cold butter, and perhaps a spoonful of my blackcurrant jam (page 32) or a good trickle of honey, or with cheese and ham as suggested here.

MAKES 1 LARGE LOAF

250g (9oz) plain flour

2 heaped teaspoons baking powder

1 teaspoon fine salt

150g (5½oz) rinded goat's cheese, cubed

50g (1¾oz) shelled hazelnuts, bashed

100g (3½oz) blackcurrants, topped and tailed

2 rosemary sprigs, roughly chopped

200ml (7fl oz) whey or buttermilk

2 tablespoons jumbo oats

Heat the oven to 200°C/400°F/gas mark 6.

In a large bowl combine the flour with the baking powder and salt, two-thirds of the goat's cheese, two-thirds of the bashed hazelnuts, the blackcurrants, chopped rosemary, and whey or buttermilk. Use your hands to form the dough into a round, about 20cm (8in) in diameter. Line a baking tray with baking parchment, place the dough round on top, then scatter over the remaining nuts and cheese, and then lastly the oats.

Cut the traditional deep cross into the surface of the dough. This will help the bread to rise. Place the bread in the oven and bake for 30–35 minutes or until well-risen and golden on top.

Serve warm from the oven with butter, a few slices of cheese and some good ham.

oat & seed flapjacks

My daughters loved making these flapjacks with their Nannar – it was an almost guaranteed activity if they went to stay up at the house. When I'd arrive to pick up the girls, the flapjacks either would be cooling in the tray beside the Rayburn or would have already been cut and placed in the flapjack tin that sat on the shelf with the rest of the tins (tins for crisps, tins for biscuits, tins for tea...). The flapjacks were always a distraction away from being too sticky and the anticipation of a child away from being too hard. Sometimes there were seeds, other times not. This recipe is my interpretation of a recipe that has never been written down. The girls and I have agreed they're pretty close to the real thing.

MAKES ABOUT 12

150g (5½oz) butter, plus extra for greasing

4 tablespoons golden syrup

75g (2½oz) soft brown sugar

250g (9oz) porridge oats

4 tablespoons mixed seeds, including pumpkin, sunflower, flaxseeds and sesame

Heat the oven to 170°C/325°F/gas mark 5 and grease a 20 x 30cm (8 x 12in) baking tray.

Place the butter, golden syrup and brown sugar in a large heavy-based pan. Heat gently, stirring often, until the butter and sugar have just melted, about 3–4 minutes. Remove the pan from the heat and pour in the porridge oats and two-thirds of the seeds. Mix everything together well with a wooden spoon.

Turn the mixture out onto the prepared baking tray, spread it evenly and level it out with a rubber spatula. Scatter over the remaining seeds and place in the oven for 18–20 minutes until golden.

Run a knife around the edge of the tin to release the flapjack. Score the surface of the flapjack into fingers or squares, but leave them in the baking tray to cool before turning them out onto a board and dividing them properly. The flapjacks will keep in an airtight container for a couple of weeks.

fig & seville marmalade breakfast buns

These breakfast buns were inspired by a winter trifle I make with dried figs and thick-cut bitter marmalade – and custard and cream, of course! I knew figs and marmalade went together well, so I tinkered with other ways I could combine them, and came up with these. Alice took a big tray of them along to her pottery class where they received such overwhelming praise (this is second-hand information, but I believe it) that I wrote the recipe down. They are absolutely perfect with a cup of coffee.

MAKES 9

500g (1lb 2oz) strong white bread flour, plus extra for dusting

75g (2½oz) caster sugar or vanilla sugar

1 teaspoon instant dried yeast

10g (¼oz) salt

200ml (7fl oz) warm milk

100g (3½oz) butter, melted, plus 50g (1¾oz) very soft butter for brushing and extra for greasing

1 egg

1 jar coarse-cut Seville orange marmalade

FOR THE FRUIT FILLING

8 dried figs, roughly chopped

juice of 1 orange

First, make the fruit filling. Place the figs in a bowl, pour over the orange juice and set aside while you make the dough.

Grease a 20 x 25cm (8 x 10in) baking tray or dish. In a bowl, combine the flour, sugar, yeast and salt, then add the milk, melted butter and egg and mix to a sticky dough. Turn out onto a floured surface and knead until smooth. Wipe the bowl clean, return the dough to the bowl, cover and leave the dough to rise until doubled in size. This might take from 2–4 hours depending on how warm it is.

When the dough is ready, carefully tip it out onto a well-floured surface, and roll it out to a rectangle of about 45 x 30cm (17½ x 12in), with one of the long sides facing towards you. Brush the surface of the dough with the soft butter. Spoon out all but a couple of tablespoons of marmalade over the top of the butter, then sprinkle over the soaked, chopped figs. Leave a margin of 2.5cm (1in) along the edge farthest away from you.

Take hold of the edge closest to you and carefully roll up the dough, enveloping the marmalade and figs in a spiral as you go. Everything's quite soft at this point so you'll need to be quite careful.

Trim the ends of the roll, then cut along the length so that you have 9 equal pieces. Arrange these snugly, cut-side down, in the greased baking tray or dish. Cover the dish or place it inside a clean plastic bag and leave it in a warm place for 1–2 hours, or until risen.

Heat the oven to 200°C/400°F/gas mark 7. Once the buns are risen, bake them for about 25–30 minutes until golden. Remove from the oven and, while they're hot, brush the buns all over with the remaining marmalade. Let cool before breaking apart and serving.

VEGETARIAN

rhubarb, blood orange, toasted almonds, honey & yoghurt

'If a blood orange bled it would bleed honey.' I can't recall who said that, but I liked the idea, and perhaps somehow it inspired this recipe, one of my favourite winter fruit salads. Raw rhubarb is really crisp and zingy and needs only the lightest tempering from honey and sweet citrus to round it. If you're not a fan of yoghurt, you can leave it out, but I like the balance it brings.

SERVES 2

1 forced rhubarb stick

2 blood oranges

1 teaspoon lightly crushed fennel seeds

2–3 tablespoons runny honey

1 tablespoon flaked almonds

2–3 tablespoons thick natural yoghurt

Slice the rhubarb into rounds of about 3–4mm (⅛in) thick and place in a bowl. Peel the oranges – I do this with a knife, which removes most of the pith – and slice them into rounds around their circumference to roughly the same thickness as the rhubarb.

Add the orange slices to the rhubarb along with the crushed fennel seeds and half the runny honey. Allow to stand while you toast the almonds. Place them in a small pan and set over a medium heat. Cook gently, tossing regularly, until they have taken on a warmer, golden colour.

Arrange the orange and rhubarb slices equally over two plates. Spoon over a little yoghurt, scatter over the toasted almonds and finish by trickling over the remaining honey.

panettone gypsy toast with dark chocolate

Panettone is a sweet, enriched Italian bread. It usually contains the zest from citrus fruit and has a light, fluffy texture. For some reason it makes a good present and at Christmas literally thousands are given away as gifts. If you've received one, or think you might in the future, then you need this recipe in your life. It is one of the simplest, most delicious breakfasts I know. (Most people call this eggy bread or French toast, but I prefer calling it gypsy toast, because I like the sound of it.)

SERVES 2

2 eggs

2 tablespoons whole milk

dash of vanilla extract or paste

tiny pinch of salt

2 thick slices of panettone

1–2 tablespoons light oil, such as sunflower

1 knob of butter

a few chunks of your favourite dark chocolate

Crack the eggs into a large, shallow bowl and add the milk, vanilla and salt. Whisk everything together until well combined.

Place the two slices of panettone into the egg mixture and leave them to soak for 5 minutes, turning them once or twice during that time.

Put the oil and butter in a large non-stick frying pan over a medium heat and when the butter has melted and they're bubbling away, place the soaked panettone into the pan and fry for 1½–2 minutes, or until the underside is lovely and golden. Flip over the two slices and cook for another 1–2 minutes until the other side is looking good too. Transfer the gypsy toasts to serving plates and finish off by grating over a little of your favourite chocolate. Serve straight away.

9.45 A.M. | FEBRUARY

Jessamy & Thomas's
after the school run
No. 9

DAY

We are like daylilies
Or something cold-blooded
Asking to sit in the sun

Holding out my hands
I hope to make things the way you do
Or nearly as beautiful

Sustenance is as the airs you make
Around my family, around this hull
Down in the dappled copse or at a laid table

I feel better when I cook something
On a warm day
If we don't share, it will only be me who remembers

steamed spring vegetables with tamari, honey & sunflower seeds

A light lunch of steamed vegetables is sometimes just what I need, and with this clean assembly, I can't help feeling it will be doing me some good, too. I've used young pak choi and little carrots here, but you could also use fresh radishes, small courgettes, French beans, or thin wedges of summer cabbage. A quick-to-make dressing and some crunchy seeds work wonders.

SERVES 2

2 small pak choi

250–300g (9–10½oz) young carrots, scrubbed and tops removed

FOR THE DRESSING

1 tablespoon sesame oil

½ red chilli, deseeded and finely sliced

2 tablespoons soy sauce or tamari

1 small bunch of spring onions, trimmed and thinly sliced

1 garlic clove, peeled and grated

1 teaspoon grated ginger

1 tablespoon cider vinegar

½ tablespoon runny honey

salt and freshly ground black pepper

FOR THE SUNFLOWER SEEDS

20g (¾oz) sunflower seeds

1½ tablespoons tamari

First, make the dressing by combining all the ingredients together in a small bowl and seasoning with salt and pepper.

Then, prepare the sunflower seeds by tossing them in the tamari and placing them in a small pan over a medium heat. Toast until the tamari has dried up and the seeds are all roasty and toasty. Set aside and allow to cool while you cook the vegetables.

Steam the vegetables together until they are tender enough to take the point of a knife with ease, about 4–6 minutes. Transfer the vegetables to a warm bowl, pour over the dressing and tumble together. Divide the coated vegetables between two plates or bowls, sprinkle over the toasted seeds and serve immediately.

new potatoes & asparagus in butter & herbs

This recipe is based on the simple idea that butter and vegetables belong with each other, in the same way the shore belongs to the sea, the moon to the night, or a child to its mother. Try to find freshly dug new potatoes, and asparagus that's been cut only a day or so before cooking – you'll notice such a difference, in both flavour and texture. Be generous with the herbs, but don't worry if you can't find all the varieties listed below – a combination of mint and parsley alone will do fine.

SERVES 4

500g (1lb 2oz) new potatoes, cut into large bite-sized chunks

2 teaspoons fine salt

50g (1¾oz) butter

4 tablespoons extra-virgin olive oil

1 small bunch of parsley, leaves picked and finely chopped

1 small bunch of mint, leaves picked and finely chopped with a few leaves left whole

small bunch of chives, finely chopped with a few left long

small bunch of chervil, finely chopped with a few leaves left whole

1 tablespoon cider vinegar

24 asparagus spears, trimmed

salt and freshly ground black pepper

Place the potatoes in a large pan. Cover generously with cold water and set over a high heat. Add the salt and bring the water to the boil. Cook the potatoes for 8–15 minutes (cooking time will vary according to the variety and freshness of the potatoes), until tender.

Drain the potatoes in a colander, then return them to the pan. Add the butter, half the olive oil and half the chopped herbs. Spoon over the vinegar, then season the potatoes really well with salt and plenty of pepper. Tumble everything together to rough up the potatoes slightly, which makes everything more delicious and buttery. Cover and keep warm.

Fill another pan with water and bring the water to the boil over a high heat. Add the asparagus spears and cook for 2–4 minutes (the cooking time will vary according to the age and size of the asparagus), until tender. Drain and return to the pan. Trickle over the remaining olive oil and season well.

Scatter the warm potatoes over a large serving platter. Arrange the asparagus over the top. Finish the dish with the remaining chopped herbs, and a few whole ones, and bring to the table immediately.

radishes with aïoli & fried fish

I love this big, friendly way to serve fillets of fish. It's generous and colourful and full of curious qualities. I like the radishes cold and crisp, the fish hot and crisp and the aïoli lovely and garlicky. It's not difficult to find radishes with their tops still on, particularly in late spring. They have a delicate flavour, and are really just like a good salad leaf.

SERVES 2 AS A MAIN

2 white fish fillets (about 400g/14oz in total), such as bream, bass, pollack or whiting, skin on

2 tablespoons extra-virgin olive oil

1 large bunch of radishes (about 12) with their tops, if possible, and halved if large

lemon, for squeezing

fennel tops, torn, to serve (optional)

salt and freshly ground black pepper

FOR THE AIOLI

(This makes more than you need, but it's so delicious you won't have any problem eating it.)

2 very fresh egg yolks

2 very fresh garlic cloves, peeled and finely grated

1 or 2 thyme sprigs, leaves picked

2 small salted anchovy fillets

1 heaped teaspoon Dijon mustard

3 teaspoons lemon juice

200ml (7fl oz) extra-virgin olive oil, plus extra for trickling

200ml (7fl oz) sunflower oil

First, make the aïoli. Put all the ingredients, except the oils, into a food processor fitted with its blade attachment and whiz for 25–30 seconds. Combine the two oils in a jug. Gradually add the oil mixture through the hole in the top of the processor in a slow and steady trickle. The oil will start to emulsify with the yolks – when it's beginning to thicken, you can add the oil a little faster. If things have gone to plan, you should have a thick, glossy mayonnaise. If it's too thick, add a tablespoon of warm water to thin it slightly.

To make the dish, heat a large non-stick frying pan over a medium–high heat. Season the fish all over. Add the olive oil to the pan and when it's nice and hot add the fish, skin-side down. Cook the fillets for 5–6 minutes, until each fillet has cooked at least three-quarters of the way up its edge and its skin is crisp. Flip the fish and cook for a further 1 minute, then remove the pan from the heat.

Divide the radishes equally between two plates. Season them with salt, pepper and a squeeze of the lemon. Cut or break up the fried fish, then arrange over the radishes. Spoon over a healthy serving of aïoli, trickle with extra-virgin olive oil and squeeze over some more lemon juice. Fennel tops are particularly good scattered over this dish just before serving, if you like.

cockles in butter & chives

The Latin word for things that are connected to the heart is *cardium*. It's the same word used to group the cockle genus. Perhaps it's the shape of their corrugated grey shells that's earned them this name, or perhaps it's got more to do with the hard-working muscle inside, the one we so love to eat. Maybe Molly Malone could tell us the answer, she certainly knew a lot about cockles and mussels. I've always enjoyed cooking and eating cockles. At their best they are sweet, plump, meaty and full of character. The adornment of vinegar, although popular, does not do this wonderful bivalve justice. They are, without question, as versatile as the mussel, and they are equally easy to cook. So, think cockles next time you plan to cook mussels, and warm a few hearts on the way.

SERVES 2

1 shallot, thinly sliced

2 bay leaves

1 thyme sprig

about 800g (1lb 12 oz) live cockles in their shells, rinsed and any open or cracked shells discarded

100g (3½oz) unsalted butter, cubed

1 bunch of chives, finely chopped

squeeze of lemon juice

salt and freshly ground black pepper

Set a large heavy-based pan over a medium–high heat. Pour in 150ml (5fl oz) of water, add the shallot, bay and thyme and bring to the boil. Add the cockles to the pan, give it a good shake and place a tight-fitting lid on top. Steam the cockles for about 2 minutes, keeping an eye on them the whole time. As soon as the shells have popped open, pour the contents of the pan into a colander set over a large bowl to collect all the wonderful cooking liquor. When the cockles are cool enough to handle, remove the cockle meat from the shells – I like to leave a few in place to garnish the dish.

Discard the bay and thyme, then pour all but the last few spoonfuls of cockle cooking liquor (the dregs may be gritty) slowly from the bowl into a clean small pan. Set it over a medium–high heat, bring to a simmer and reduce to a scant 150ml (5fl oz). With the pan still over the heat, add the butter and stir it well. When the butter is melted and the sauce is hot, stir in the chives and a squeeze of lemon juice and season with black pepper. Taste the sauce – it shouldn't need salt, but you can add a pinch now if it does. Add the cockle meat, stir once or twice to heat through, then take the pan off the heat.

If you've left a few cockles in the shells, divide these between two bowls. Spoon over the cockles and hot buttery sauce and serve with fresh crusty bread and a salad, or some sliced ripe tomatoes dressed with extra-virgin olive oil, salt and red wine vinegar.

rhubarb & cicely jelly

Some of the best jellies are sharp things we've made sweet. Take lemon jelly as an example. A good one will make you shudder and smile at the same time. Rhubarb makes a gorgeous jelly: its sour, fruity juice is perfect for it. Cicely, a herb I like to use in the spring and summer, works really nicely with rhubarb. It's sugary on the tongue, giving it a natural sweetness that means you can cut back the refined sugar content a little. I like to serve the jelly with a scattering of this sweet green herb over the top and some candied raw rhubarb sticks on the side.

MAKES 4 JELLIES

6 bright, fresh rhubarb stems, trimmed and cut into 2–3cm (¾–1¼in) pieces

175g (6oz) granulated sugar

1 small bunch of sweet cicely, plus a few extra flowers to decorate

up to 4 sheets of gelatin

FOR THE CANDIED RHUBARB

4 very young rhubarb stalks (or 1 larger one cut into long, thin sticks)

1–2 teaspoons runny honey

1 tablespoon granulated sugar

Place the rhubarb in a large heavy-based pan along with the sugar, sweet cicely and 400ml (14fl oz) of water. Set the pan over a medium heat and bring the liquid to a gentle simmer, stirring once or twice to help break down the rhubarb a little. Cook gently for 6–8 minutes, or until the rhubarb is pulpy and everything smells lovely and fragrant. Switch off the heat and allow the liquid to cool to room temperature. This gives the cicely the maximum time to infuse.

Once the rhubarb has cooled, pass the juice through a sieve lined with a piece of muslin or thin cotton cloth. You can either leave it to drip through of its own accord or you can gather up the cloth and encourage every last drop out by squeezing gently.

You should have about 500ml (17fl oz) of liquid. Soak the correct amount of gelatin sheets to set that quantity of liquid (usually about four leaves, but check the packet instructions) in cold water for 2–3 minutes until soft.

Put the rhubarb juice in a clean pan and warm it through to just below boiling point. Add the soaked gelatin leaves, and stir well to dissolve. Pour the jelly into moulds or glasses, or as I have here, onto a relatively deep plate. Carefully place the jellies in the fridge and leave for at least 1 hour to set.

Before serving, make the candied rhubarb. Brush the little rhubarb stems with some runny honey, then roll them in the sugar to coat. To serve, set these tangy canes down next to the jelly, which you can, if you have them, scatter with some cicely flowers.

12.30 P.M. | JUNE

Tania & Alex's
from a sunny garden
The Mill

summer garden tart

Another of my assemblies, this tart is open to interpretation, alteration and variation. I've simply taken everything that is green and good from the garden and piled it onto puff pastry, which I'd suggest is a most suitable vessel. Without the pastry this would become a light and delicate salad, and one with absolute merit. On toast, you would have a colourful bruschetta – or in a broth of light chicken stock, a beautiful garden soup. The quantities here are a guide for you. If broad beans aren't your favourite, you could use asparagus. Peppery rocket would make a great alternative to the nasturtiums I'm using; and when it comes to herbs, it really is your call.

SERVES 4

1 sheet of good-quality, ready-rolled puff pastry (about 25cm x 15cm/10in x 6in)

3 or 4 small–medium courgettes, trimmed and sliced into 1cm (½in) thick rounds

zest and juice of ½ lemon

4 tablespoons extra-virgin olive oil

300g (10½oz) broad beans in the pod, podded

2–3 handfuls of super-fresh peas in the pod (or use frozen peas)

about 100g (3½oz) feta cheese

4–6 spring onions, trimmed and sliced

a little of each of the following prepared herbs, if available: chives (leaves and flowers), fennel (tops and flowers), mint leaves, nasturtium leaves, thyme leaves

salt and freshly ground black pepper

Heat the oven to 180°C/350°F/gas mark 6. Line a baking tray large enough to hold your puff pastry sheet with baking parchment. Place the pastry on top and gently score a 2cm (¾in) margin all the way around the edge of the pastry. Place the tray in the oven and bake the pastry for 18–25 minutes, or until puffed up and golden. Remove from the oven and carefully press down the pastry within the scored margin. It will break and crack a bit but this is what you want.

Heat the grill to hot. Scatter the courgettes over a large baking tray. Season them well with salt and pepper, scatter over the lemon zest and trickle over half the olive oil. Turn the courgette slices to coat, then arrange them in a single layer over the tray. Place the courgettes under the grill for about 6–8 minutes, turning once, until golden and blistered on both sides. Remove and allow to cool a little.

Bring a small pan of water to the boil and cook the broad beans and peas for 2–3 minutes, until tender. Drain and allow to cool. Pop any larger beans out of their skins, as they can be a little tough. Season the beans and peas with a little salt and pepper, a squeeze of lemon and half the remaining olive oil.

To assemble, scatter the courgettes over the base of the pastry case. Crumble over half the cheese randomly, then scatter over the peas, beans and spring onions. Add the remaining cheese, then strew over the herb flowers and leaves. Give everything a trickle with the remaining olive oil and finish with a final spritz of lemon juice before serving. This is wonderful with a lemon mayonnaise (page 220).

cos lettuces with tarragon dressing & hard goat's cheese

This dressing, which is really what this salad is all about, was inspired by something I can't quite remember eating in Berlin. The depth of it and the overall joy it brings comes from sweet, green tarragon, one of my favourite herbs. It gets puréed with natural yoghurt, which I find intensely delicious. I've used cos lettuce, much loved for its crunchy, cool nature, but you could use a softer butterhead. Something goaty to finish works well with the tarragon, but that's not to say it wouldn't be equally good with an aged sheep's cheese.

SERVES 4

2 crisp cos lettuce

75g (2½oz) hard goat's or sheep's cheese, finely grated

FOR THE DRESSING

2 teaspoons Dijon mustard

3 teaspoons cider vinegar

2 teaspoons unrefined golden caster sugar

2 tablespoons natural yoghurt

50ml (1¾fl oz) sunflower oil

50ml (1¾fl oz) extra-virgin olive oil

bunch of tarragon, leaves stripped

salt and freshly ground black pepper

Remove the base from the lettuce with a sharp knife, then separate the leaves. Slice the longer ones into shorter lengths, then wash all the leaves and spin them dry.

To make the dressing, put all the ingredients (except a scattering of tarragon leaves) into a jug blender, season with salt and pepper, and blitz everything together until the tarragon is finely chopped and the dressing is lovely and thick. Set aside.

Pile the cos leaves into a big salad bowl and drench all over with the dressing. Sprinkle the grated cheese over the top of the dressed leaves and finish with the reserved tarragon.

elderflower cordial

The rites of June: sea swimming, elderflower cordial (a prayer to the sun).

MAKES ABOUT 2 LITRES

36 large heads of elderflower

juice and finely grated zest of 4 unwaxed lemons (you should have about 150ml/5fl oz juice in total)

1 lemon, sliced into thin rounds

750g (1lb 10oz) unrefined golden caster sugar

250g (9oz) runny honey

1 teaspoon citric acid (optional)

Inspect the elderflower heads and remove any insects that might have found a home in them. Place the heads in a large, clean bowl together with the grated lemon zest and the sliced lemon.

Bring 1.5 litres (52fl oz) of water to the boil in a large pan, remove the pan from the heat and pour the water over the elderflowers. Stir once or twice, cover and leave overnight to infuse.

Strain the infused liquid through a scalded jelly bag or piece of clean muslin into a large jug, then pour the liquid into a large pan (you can use the pan you used for boiling the water). Add the sugar, honey, lemon juice, and citric acid, if using.

Place the pan over a low heat and heat the liquid gently, just enough to dissolve the honey and citric acid, but don't let it boil.

Use a funnel to pour the hot cordial into sterilized bottles (see page 32). Seal the bottles with swing-top lids, sterilized screw-tops or corks. The cordial will keep for several weeks in the fridge.

chilled kohlrabi, courgette & kefir soup

I've tried not to lose the kohlrabi's delicate, subtle flavour in this chilled summer soup. As long as you make it with care, all the flavours will come through, even when it's cold. I find the acidity from the kefir milk (a fermented milk, not unlike yoghurt, and readily available) key to this. Not only is it delicious, but it also helps to accentuate the soup's gentle flavours, in the same way lemon might.

SERVES 2–3

2 tablespoons extra-virgin olive oil

2 large courgettes, trimmed and thinly sliced

1 onion, halved and sliced

2 garlic cloves, peeled and thinly sliced

1 large kohlrabi, peeled and cut into small cubes

350ml (12fl oz) well-flavoured vegetable stock

small handful of mint leaves

small handful of dill, plus extra chopped dill to serve

150ml (5fl oz) milk kefir or natural yoghurt, chilled

good-quality extra-virgin olive oil, to serve

salt and freshly ground black pepper

Place a large heavy-based pan over a medium heat. Add the olive oil followed by the sliced courgettes, onion and garlic and cubed kohlrabi. Sweat the vegetables gently, stirring regularly, for 10–15 minutes, until everything is soft, but has not taken on any colour. Pour in the vegetable stock and bring the liquid up to the simmer. Turn down the heat and place a lid on the pan. Cook for a further 15 minutes, until the vegetables are lovely and soft.

Take the soup off the heat and pour into a jug blender. Add the mint and dill, and season with some salt and pepper, then whiz to a smooth consistency. Taste the soup and adjust the seasoning, remembering to add a pinch more salt than you might think necessary, as the flavours are muted when the soup is chilled. Place the soup in the fridge to chill completely.

When you're ready to serve, stir in the chilled milk kefir or yoghurt, pour into chilled bowls and serve straight away with a trickle of best-quality olive oil and a scattering of chopped dill.

pickled cucumbers with dill & oak

If you like pickles and ferments, then you have to make these – they are amazing! Try to find fresh little cucumbers that smell sweet and are firm to the touch, as these will give you pickles with the best flavour. I like to spike the salty brine with dill, mustard seeds, sliced red onions and a touch of garlic. And I find adding a few oak leaves to the jar really helps the cucumbers retain that all-important crunch, thanks to the tannins in the leaves. If you can't find an oak tree in leaf, you can use blackcurrant leaves instead. These cucumbers are insane with grilled steak, shellfish, good cheese, fatty charcuterie, or anything smoked or straight out of the fire.

FILLS A 2-LITRE (70FL OZ)
KILNER JAR

10–12 small, firm, exceptionally fresh cucumbers

1 small red onion, thinly sliced

1 bunch of dill, with flowering tops, if possible

6–8 oak leaves, or blackcurrant leaves if you can't find oak

2 garlic cloves, bashed, skin on

1 tablespoon black mustard seeds

40g (1½oz) fine salt

Cut the flowering tops from the cucumbers if they have them, then give them a gentle wash in iced water. Leave them to sit in the water for 15–20 minutes.

Drain the cucumbers and pack them into a clean 2-litre (70fl oz) Kilner jar (seal removed), along with the onion, dill, oak or blackcurrant leaves, garlic cloves and mustard seeds.

Put 1 litre (35fl oz) of water in a large jug and add the salt. Whisk thoroughly to dissolve and create a brine.

Pour the brine into the jar. Fill a small plastic food bag with water and sit this on top of the cucumbers and other ingredients. This will keep everything submerged below the salty brine.

Close the lid. Leave the jar in a cool place for 4–5 days to allow the cucumbers to ferment. Lift the lid and remove a cucumber. Have a taste; it should have a real tang and funk to its flavour. If you're happy with the taste, you can pop the jar in the fridge. Consume the pickles within a year.

1.15 P.M. | AUGUST

Polly's gran's life
Lyme Regis

chicken with chamomile

There is a place between asleep and awake where our bodies are unneeded and we remember dreaming. It's a stilling state that's difficult to attain, but perhaps this beautiful chicken broth, gently flavoured with fresh chamomile flowers might help us get there. What could be more sedative or lulling? If you can't find fresh chamomile flowers, you can use dried to flavour the broth. They work in the same way, but you won't need quite as many.

SERVES 2

500ml (17fl oz) chicken stock
(see below)

1 chicken breast

10–14 chamomile flowers

squeeze of lemon juice

salt and freshly ground
black pepper

FOR THE CHICKEN STOCK
(MAKES 1–1.5 LITRES/
35–52FL OZ)

2 freshly roasted chicken
carcasses, and any other bits left
in the roasting tray

1–2 onions, sliced

2 large carrots, roughly chopped

3–4 celery sticks, roughly
chopped

½ leek, roughly sliced

2 or 3 garlic cloves, peeled
and bashed

6 thyme sprigs

a few parsley stalks

3 or 4 bay leaves

1 teaspoon black peppercorns

First, make the chicken stock. Tear the carcasses into several pieces and pack them, along with any skin, fat, jelly, bones or other tasty morsels from the roasting tray into a large pan. Add all the vegetables, as well as the herbs and peppercorns, packing them in nice and neatly. Pour over 1.5 litres (52fl oz) of water to cover. Place the pan over a medium heat and bring up to a very gentle simmer. Reduce the heat to low and continue to simmer gently, uncovered, for 2–3 hours, topping up the water during cooking, if necessary. Pass the cooked stock through a very fine sieve lined with a piece of muslin or a clean cotton cloth, into a clean bowl or container. Allow to cool, then cover and refrigerate until you're ready to use it.

To make the dish, remove any fat from the surface of the chilled stock. Pour 500ml (17fl oz) of the stock into a medium pan and set it over a medium–high heat. Bring the stock to a gentle simmer. Place the chicken breast into the pan with the stock, cover with a lid and cook gently for 10–12 minutes, or until the chicken is just cooked through. Use a slotted spoon to remove the chicken from the pan and leave it to rest somewhere warm. Taste the stock in the pan as it simmers away, and season with plenty of salt and pepper – it should be full of flavour.

Divide the chamomile flowers between two warmed bowls. Cut the warm chicken into thin slices and place it next to the flowers. Ladle over the simmering stock and finish with a tiny squeeze of lemon juice over each serving before bringing to the table.

gooseberry, bacon & camembert rough-edged tart

The gooseberry is a member of the *Ribes* family, which includes black, red and white currants. Anything called *Ribes* is okay with me; it's such a brilliant word and we should all be eating more of this versatile little fruit during its shortish season. Gooseberries are delicious raw in salsas and salads, cooked in sugary compôtes, sorbets and ice cream, or pickled and preserved in chutneys and jam. Here, I use ripe gooseberries just as you would cherry tomatoes (they have very similar qualities) with Camembert and salty bacon. I make my pastry with rye flour, which gives it a nutty, crumbly texture.

SERVES 6

2 tablespoons porridge oats

about 450g (1lb) ripe gooseberries

150g (5½oz) streaky bacon

150g (5½oz) Camembert, thickly sliced

a few thyme sprigs

2–3 tablespoons runny honey

1 egg, beaten

salt and freshly ground black pepper

FOR THE RYE SHORT CRUST

100g (3½oz) rye flour

200g (7oz) plain flour, plus extra for serving

150g (5½oz) butter, cubed and chilled

pinch of fine salt

First, make the rye short crust. Place the flours, butter and salt in a food processor and pulse until you have a breadcrumb consistency. Then, with the motor turning, gradually add 2–4 tablespoons of water until everything begins to come together. Stop the machine, remove the pastry, and knead it a couple of times before wrapping it in cling-film and chilling it in the fridge for at least 30 minutes.

Heat the oven to 200°C/400°F/gas mark 7.

To make the tart, first remove the pastry from the fridge and leave to stand at room temperature for 30 minutes. Then, roll out the pastry on a cool, floured surface to a round of about 40cm (16in) in diameter and about 2–3mm (1/16–1/8in) thick. Slide the pastry onto a large piece of baking parchment, then slide the parchment onto a large baking sheet.

Sprinkle the porridge oats over the middle of the pastry, leaving a 6–7cm (2½–2¾in) margin around the edge. The oats will absorb some of the gooseberry juices, keeping the pastry lovely and crisp. Arrange the gooseberries in a generous pile on top of the oats. Roughly tear the bacon rashers and lay these evenly over the berries. Top with the slices of cheese and the thyme sprigs. Trickle runny honey over the whole lot and season with salt and pepper. Fold over the sides of the pastry to enclose the edges of the filling and brush the pastry with the beaten egg. Place the tart in the oven and bake for 35–40 minutes or until the pastry is beautifully golden, the bacon is crisp and the gooseberries are tender. Serve warm.

grilled squid with broad beans, mint, lemon & agretti

If you don't have a ridged grill pan for this recipe, use a heavy-based frying pan instead. The trick in either case is to get the pan really, really hot, so the squid cooks quickly and retains its soft, tender texture. Agretti, sometimes known as monk's beard, is a popular Italian vegetable. It's a frondy member of the samphire family, and although it has a slight salinity, its flavour is close to that of spinach. You can eat young shoots raw in salads, but as the shoots get bigger, they benefit from blanching (just like broad beans). Mint, chives and a little parsley are lovely herbs to use for this recipe, if you have them to hand.

SERVES 2

4 small or 2 medium squid (about 400g/14oz in total), cleaned

2 tablespoons extra-virgin olive oil

250g (9oz) small broad beans, shelled

1 small bunch of agretti (about 60g/2¼oz; optional)

1 small knob of butter

1 small garlic clove, peeled and grated or finely chopped

½ small handful of mint leaves, finely ribboned

½ small bunch of chives, finely chopped

a few stems of flat-leaf parsley, leaves picked

lemon, for squeezing

salt and freshly ground black pepper

Use a sharp knife to cut the tubular body of each squid down its length, so it completely opens up. Then, use a blunt knife to score the inside, in a cross-hatch pattern. If you're using larger squid, cut each body into two or three pieces. Put the scored squid in a bowl along with the wings and tentacles (you might want to halve these) and season it all with salt and pepper. Trickle over 1 tablespoon of the olive oil and tumble everything together.

Heat a large, ridged griddle pan over a very high heat and bring a large pan of salted water to the boil. Once the griddle pan is madly hot, add the squid. Cook for around 45–60 seconds on each side. Remove the squid from the griddle and transfer to a plate.

Add the beans and agretti to the pan of boiling water and cook for 1–3 minutes, depending on the size and age of the broad beans. (Larger, older beans might benefit from skinning once cooked.) Drain the broad beans and agretti and set aside.

Add the butter to the drained cooking pan, with the remaining olive oil and the garlic. Let the garlic sizzle over a low heat for 30 seconds, then return the agretti and beans to the pan, stirring them through the garlic butter. Remove from the heat and stir through half each of the mint, chives and parsley. Season with salt and pepper.

Arrange the beans and agretti over two warm plates, top each with the grilled squid and then with the remaining herbs. Finish each with a squeeze of lemon juice.

crayfish salad with radishes, apple, poppy seeds & soured cream

I remember catching crayfish in traps that had been set around the edges of a lake in Dorset. I recall how plucky and determined these little freshwater lobsters were. They raised their small claws in the air to scare me off and they nipped at me when I went near. They were determined not to accompany me home. Crayfish meat is sweet and juicy and absolutely delicious served simply with brown bread, butter, dill and lemon. But if you're feeling more adventurous, this quick and scrumptious salad with crunchy radish, sharp apples and the toothsome bite of poppy seeds showcases crayfish beautifully.

SERVES 4

big bunch of radishes
(about 16 radishes)

2 small dessert apples

about 400g (14oz) crayfish meat

juice of ½ lemon

2 tablespoons extra-virgin
olive oil

1 small bunch of mint, leaves
picked and chopped

½ small bunch of dill chopped,
plus a few extra sprigs to
decorate

2–3 teaspoons poppy seeds

FOR THE DRESSING

juice of ½ lemon

2 teaspoons sugar

2 teaspoons soured cream

2 teaspoons extra-virgin olive oil

salt and freshly ground
black pepper

Trim and wash the radishes. If they have their green tops on and they're in good condition, you can use them in the salad. If not, don't worry. Slice the radishes into nice, thin rounds, about 2–3mm (1/16–1/8in) thick.

Peel, quarter and core the apple, then slice each quarter thinly.

Place the crayfish meat in a large bowl with the radish and apple slices. Pour over the lemon juice, spoon over the olive oil and scatter over the chopped herbs. Season well with salt and pepper, then gently tumble everything together.

To make the dressing, put all the ingredients in a small bowl, season well with salt and pepper, and whisk or mix well to combine.

Arrange the salad over four plates or one large serving platter, spoon equal amounts of the dressing over each serving, then scatter over the poppy seeds. Finish with a few sprigs of dill.

fresh crab on toast with fenugreek, chilli, eggs & olive oil

There are a few things I like to eat more than anything else in this life. One such being fresh crab – on toast, with a good mayonnaise. It's something I always hope to find on my 'last supper' table. This recipe is a riff on that, but essentially the crab is still on toast. If you haven't tasted fenugreek before, I'd urge you to do so. If you haven't had it with crab, then here's your chance. As spices go, it is quite unique. It has a warmth and a smokiness, and then an almost bitter quality that does wonderful things with the sweet crab meat. I like to set everything out on the table, so people can help themselves.

SERVES 4–6

2 large live brown cock crabs, about 1kg (2lb 4oz) each

4 eggs, at room temperature

1 hot red chilli, halved, deseeded and very thinly sliced

1 small garlic clove, peeled and sliced into very fine slivers

1 teaspoon crushed fenugreek seeds

5 tablespoons extra-virgin olive oil

2 tablespoons mayonnaise

lemon, for squeezing

8–12 slices of sourdough or good-quality rustic bread, toasted and buttered, to serve

salt and freshly ground black pepper

You must kill the crabs before cooking, as it's the most humane way to treat them. Lay each crab on its back and lift the tail flap to reveal a cone-shaped indentation in the shell. Quickly push a sharp spike, nail or bradle into this indent and twist a couple of times to sever tissues in the ventral nerve centre. Then immediately drive the spike into the crab's head, through the mouth, between and below the eyes, and lever it back and forth a few times to destroy the nerve tissues here.

To cook the crabs, bring a large pan of well-salted water to the boil. Place the crabs into the boiling water. Once boiling again, cook for 10–12 minutes. (I allow 1 minute for roughly every 100g/3½oz the crab weighs.) Take the crabs out of the pan and leave to cool. Discard the cooking water.

To pick the meat from your crabs, first twist off the legs and claws. Open the body by pulling the undercarriage away from the shell: press your thumb onto the face of each crab, just below the eyes – the undercarriage will crack and pop inwards. Lift this up and out of the shell and discard. You're left with the rich and creamy brown meat (the texture can vary depending on the condition of the crab). Use a pick or teaspoon to remove all the meat from the shell and set aside.

Discard the grey feathery gills (or 'dead man's fingers') from the body. Cut the body in half down the middle and pick out the delicate white meat; the meat runs right through into the joint of each leg.

continues >

Lightly crack the legs and claws using the back of a heavy knife or a small hammer. You'll find the majority of the white meat in the front claws, but take your time with the legs, as it's surprising how much meat you can amass. Once you've picked off all the white meat, set it aside while you prepare the remaining ingredients.

To cook the eggs, bring a medium pan of water to the boil. Carefully add the eggs to the water, bring back to the boil and cook for 6½ minutes to hard boil. Drain the eggs, then run them under a cold tap for a minute or so, to stop them cooking. Peel the eggs and set them aside.

Place the chilli and garlic in a small pan with the fenugreek and 4 tablespoons of the olive oil. Set the pan over a low heat and cook gently until the garlic is fragrant, but not coloured; about 3–4 minutes. Remove the pan from the heat and allow to cool.

Place the brown crab meat on a board, add the mayonnaise, a good squeeze of lemon juice, the remaining spoonful of olive oil and plenty of salt and pepper. Use a knife to chop all this together until everything is well mixed and the meat is relatively fine.

To serve, spread the buttered toast with a generous spoonful of dressed brown crab meat, followed by some white. Halve or quarter the eggs and arrange a few pieces over the crab. Trickle over a teaspoon of the chilli and fenugreek oil and finish with another squeeze of lemon.

barbecued mackerel with black pudding & redcurrants

Catch the life as it runs and stew it up in grain. Pay the toll. Make the fire up and blacken the fish, blacken the blood, take the fruit from its cage.

SERVES 4

4 mackerel, filleted, skin on

2 tablespoons extra-virgin olive oil

a few rosemary sprigs

200g (7oz) black pudding, sliced into nice, thick rounds

3 or 4 small bay leaves

lemon, for squeezing

150g (5½oz) white or redcurrants

salt and freshly ground black pepper

Light the barbecue and allow the charcoal to burn down to a nice even, high heat (it's ready when you can hover your hand over the grill for only 1–2 seconds).

Place the fillets of mackerel on a large plate. Trickle over the olive oil, tear over the rosemary and season them all over with salt and pepper. Turn the fillets through the oil and seasoning to coat.

Lay the mackerel fillets skin-side down on the barbecue grill. Arrange the slices of black pudding around these; chuck on the rosemary and bay for good measure.

Grill the fish, skin-side down, until it is almost cooked through – you can tell when to flip it, because the translucent pink flesh will turn opaque, about 2–3 minutes over a hot fire.

While the fish is cooking, turn the black pudding once or twice, you want it to begin to crisp around its edges.

Flip the mackerel and cook for a further 25–30 seconds, before removing the fillets to a large, warm plate. Lift the black pudding from the grill and roughly break it over the fish. Squeeze some lemon juice over the berries, then scatter the berries over the plate. Serve at once with hunks of bread.

fried mackerel with tomatoes, garlic & herbs

I really like this. For me as a cook (and someone who loves food), it embodies everything I believe in and is right. These ingredients are honest, we can trust they will be good – if we treat them kindly: from the sea kindly, out of the earth kindly, in the pan kindly.

SERVES 2

150–200g (5½–7oz) ripe cherry tomatoes, on or off the vine

2 bay leaves

3 or 4 thyme sprigs

2 large marjoram sprigs

2 or 3 garlic cloves, peeled and sliced

2 tablespoons extra-virgin olive oil

1 knob of butter

1 large mackerel, filleted, skin on

salt and freshly ground black pepper

Heat the oven to 200°C/400°F/gas mark 7.

Place the tomatoes in a small roasting tin or baking tray with the herbs, garlic and olive oil and season well with salt and pepper.

Place in the hot oven and cook for 15–20 minutes, until the tomatoes are splitting and lightly blistered. Remove from the oven and set aside.

Heat a medium non-stick frying pan over a medium–high heat. Add the butter, then the two mackerel fillets, skin-side down. Cook for 2–3 minutes, until the fillets are almost cooked through, then flip the fish over and switch off the heat. The fillets will cook through in the residual heat of the pan.

Divide the roasted tomatoes equally between two warm plates, then serve the mackerel alongside, trickled with a spoonful or two of the herby, garlicky juices.

hot-smoked mackerel

Hot smoking your own mackerel fillets makes the pre-packed, shop-bought versions pale into realms less interesting (although they themselves can sometimes be good). Eating just-cooked fillets straight from the smoker is a true pleasure. When they are warm, moist and smoky, they are extraordinary, and anyone who appreciates how good fresh mackerel can be should add this to their armoury of cooking techniques. I've made hot smokers out of biscuit tins, saucepans, deep roasting trays and even the old enamel bread tins you can sometimes find at car boots or charity shops. These are particularly good, as you can get a couple of racks inside, one above the other. As long as your chosen vessel is in no way flammable, and has a lid and a solid base, it can be customized for the job. Use hardwood shavings or chips and avoid resinous or sappy woods. As a general rule, any tree that produces fruit or nuts for us to eat lends itself to smoking. If you know a joiner, or there is a joinery workshop in your area, get down and see them. They usually have an excess of hardwood shavings they can't give away.

300g (10½oz) fine sea salt
6 fresh mackerel fillets, skin on
coarsely cracked black pepper

To start off the process you need to lightly salt the fillets.

Take a large plastic tray and scatter it all over with a fine layer of sea salt. Lay the mackerel fillets skin-side down over the salt. Scatter another layer of salt on top, making sure all the fish gets some salt. Repeat this process if you have more fish to use – just layer them up.

Leave the fillets to salt for 15–20 minutes, then gently wash off the salt under a cold running tap. Pat the fillets dry thoroughly with kitchen paper or a clean tea towel, then sprinkle the fish with some coarsely cracked black pepper.

Set up your hot smoker. (It's well worth practising with it before you actually use it for real.) Place the smoker over your chosen heat source, add the wood shavings or chips and bring it up to heat. (At home I use my Green Egg to smoke things in – the principle is the same.) Lay the fish on the rack and pop on the lid. Smoke the fish over a medium heat for 8–10 minutes, or until just cooked through – the flesh should flake from the skin.

Serve the smoked fish simply, with buttered slices of bread, drizzled with a squeeze of lemon juice, and a spoonful of horesradish on the side. Alternatively use them as in the recipe on page 140.

runner beans with hot-smoked mackerel, horseradish & tarragon

I wasn't overly interested in runner beans as a child; they were always in my periphery. I did, however, like the old turquoise, crank-handled, runner-bean slicer my mum used to get out to prepare them. (People like anything you put something in, and it comes out looking different.) I found the turquoise slicer sinister, although it drew me in, as red jam to a wasp, to turn the handle, to test it, to slice... things. These days I love runner beans, but I use a sharp knife to slice them. I like them cut thinly and on the angle. When they are young and fresh, they are divine simply buttered, but this salad of smoked mackerel, peppy horseradish and sweet tarragon offers an altogether different way to enjoy them.

SERVES 2

200g (7oz) runner beans (stringy bits removed), sliced thinly at an angle

2 tablespoons extra-virgin olive oil

1 tablespoon chopped tarragon leaves

4 hot-smoked mackerel fillets (see page 136)

FOR THE HORSERADISH & TARRAGON DRESSING

1 tablespoon horseradish sauce

1 teaspoon Dijon mustard

2 teaspoons crème fraîche

juice of ½ lemon

1 teaspoon red wine vinegar

1 tablespoon chopped tarragon

½ teaspoon caster sugar

salt and freshly ground black pepper

First, make the dressing. Combine all the dressing ingredients together and season with salt and pepper to taste. The dressing should be hot, sharp and sweet all at the same time. Set aside.

To make the dish, bring a pan of salted water to the boil. Cook the runner beans for 3–4 minutes, until just tender. Drain the beans and dress them with the olive oil and some chopped tarragon.

Flake the mackerel flesh into large chunks, discarding the skin, and tumble the fish together with the warm beans and half the dressing. Transfer to a salad bowl, trickle over the remaining dressing and scatter over the rest of the tarragon. Serve straight away.

raspberries in elderflower syrup with crushed meringue & elderflower petals

Soft red fruits, such as raspberries, are lovely with elderflower. They seem to have a natural affinity. In June, when the creamy, white flowers are in full flush, I like to finish this salad with a scattering of elderflower petals. They are minute, and often dusty with pollen, but ever-so pretty. However, when the flowers die back in July, you can just leave them out, as a lot of the flavour is in the syrup itself.

SERVES 2

2 egg whites

100g (3½oz) unrefined caster sugar

250g (9oz) raspberries

3 tablespoons elderflower cordial (see page 112)

1 or 2 small sprays of freshly picked elderflowers (optional)

Begin by making the meringue. Heat the oven to 120°C/235°F/gas mark 1. Ensure that the bowl of your kitchen mixer is completely clean, add the egg whites and whisk on a medium speed until they form soft peaks. With the motor still running, gradually add the caster sugar, 1 tablespoon at a time. Once you have added all the sugar, continue whisking for another 3–4 minutes, until the meringue is thick and glossy. (You can also make the meringue with an electric hand whisk).

Line a baking sheet with a piece of baking parchment. Spoon the mixture into four rough, heaped mounds. Place the baking sheet in the oven and bake the meringue for 25–30 minutes, then turn down the heat to 90°C/195°F/gas mark ½ and cook for a further 2 hours, until the meringues are crisp. Remove the meringues from the oven and allow to cool.

Place the raspberries in a large bowl, trickle over the elderflower cordial and carefully tumble the fruit around.

To serve, scatter the raspberries over a large plate and crush over a little meringue (you won't need all four meringues – the remainder will keep in an airtight container for up to three days, or freeze them for up to a month). Finally, scatter over the elderflower petals and serve straight away.

1.10 P.M. | SEPTEMBER

Sarah & Paul's
and everyone's before them
Hawkstone Abbey Farm

wild mushroom tart

There is a wood near the house where the trees are evergreen, carved into expanses by footpaths lined with elder, beech and oak. The ground is so soft it deadens almost all sound, even the wind. Here, mushrooms grow from late summer until early winter. On days when I return with a small haul, I make this tart – one of my absolute favourites.

SERVES 8–10

1 knob of butter

2 tablespoons extra-virgin olive oil

20g (¾oz) dried ceps, soaked for 20–25 minutes in warm water to rehydrate, then drained, soaking water reserved

250g (9oz) mushrooms, a mixture of wild and cultivated is fine

1 tablespoon chopped flat-leaf parsley

2 teaspoons thyme leaves

1 large onion, thinly sliced

2 garlic cloves, peeled and thinly sliced

185ml (6fl oz) double cream

2 eggs, plus 1 egg yolk

scattering of Parmesan or hard, aged sheep's cheese

salt and freshly ground black pepper

FOR THE SHORT CRUST

300g (10½oz) plain flour

150g (5½oz) butter, cubed and chilled

pinch of fine salt

about 150ml (5fl oz) chilled water

First, make the short crust. Pulse the flour, butter and salt in a food processor to the consistency of breadcrumbs. With the motor running, steadily add the water, stopping as soon as the dough comes together. Remove the dough, knead it a couple of times, then wrap it in cling film and chill it in the fridge for at least 30 minutes.

Heat the oven to 180°C/350°F/gas mark 6. Roll the chilled dough into a thin round large enough to line a 24cm (9½in) loose-bottomed, fluted tart tin, with an overhang. Prick the base, then line the pastry with baking parchment and baking beans and bake in the oven for about 20 minutes. Remove the parchment and beans and return to the oven for a further 5 minutes, or until the base is dry and lightly coloured. Trim any overhanging pastry from the tart and set aside.

Next, make the filling. Heat a large frying pan over a medium–high heat. Add the butter and half the oil. When the fat is bubbling away, add both the soaked and fresh mushrooms, along with the parsley and thyme. Season with salt and pepper. Toss the mushrooms around the pan and cook for 3–4 minutes, until softened. Tip the mushrooms into a large bowl, then return the pan to the heat, add the remaining oil, and the onion and garlic and fry gently for about 8–10 minutes, until the onion is soft. Add all but the last spoonful (which may be gritty) of the mushroom liquid to the onion mixture and reduce until it's almost gone. Combine the onion with the mushrooms, and season.

Put the cream, eggs and egg yolk in a bowl, season, then combine to form a custard. Fill the tart case with the onion and mushroom mixture and pour over the custard. Don't worry if a few mushrooms poke out. Scatter over a gesture of cheese and bake the tart for 30–35 minutes, until it has a mottled golden top and is slightly raised. Allow to rest for at least 20 minutes before serving.

mushroom, cider & blue cheese soup

What a collective these three ingredients turned out to be. I like the sound and sense of them together (sometimes I'll base a recipe on that alone). They all have a very natural feel, because each is the product of a craft or a passion, which requires understanding, patience and care. This makes them really special. This is an earthy, rich soup with a wonderful amount of character and a deeply savoury flavour. I like to save a few whole mushrooms to sauté and serve on top, particularly if I've picked a few of them myself.

SERVES 4–6

about 500g (1lb 2oz) wild and cultivated mushrooms

25g (1oz) butter, plus an extra knob, for frying

extra-virgin olive oil

1 leek, sliced

1 small potato, peeled and diced

1 large onion, chopped

2 garlic cloves, peeled

1 teaspoon thyme leaves

750ml (26fl oz) vegetable or chicken stock

250ml (9fl oz) dry cider

100ml (3½fl oz) double cream

75g (2½oz) blue cheese, plus a little extra to serve

1 small bunch of parsley, finely chopped, to serve

salt and freshly ground black pepper

Carefully prepare the mushrooms – you don't have to be as precious with the trimming. For example, as long as the stalks are clean and free of soil they can go in. Likewise caps that might offend in a sauté, won't once puréed. Set aside 100g (3½oz) of the most aesthetically pleasing fungi to fry off and garnish the soup at the end. Roughly chop the remainder.

Pull out your favourite soup pan, put it over a medium heat, add the butter and a splash of olive oil and allow to foam. Add the leek, potato, onion and garlic. Cook for 10–15 minutes, until the onion is soft but not coloured. Add the chopped mushrooms and thyme leaves, then season with a little salt and pepper. Cook for a further 5 minutes, then pour over the stock and cider and bring to a simmer. Cook for 12–15 minutes until everything is nice and tender. Remove from the heat and purée the soup until smooth and creamy. I find that a jug blender is the best tool for this job.

Return the soup to the pan. Add the cream and blue cheese and bring gently back to a simmer. Season to taste and keep warm on the lowest of heats.

Heat a medium frying pan over a high heat. Add a knob of butter and a splash more olive oil. Add the reserved mushrooms and sauté, tossing regularly, for 8–10 minutes, or until they are well cooked. Season the mushrooms to taste and keep warm. To serve, ladle the soup into warmed bowls and top with the fried mushrooms, a crumbling of blue cheese, a scattering of chopped parsley and a crack of black pepper.

quinoa salad with roasted squash, kale, walnuts, garlic & red-wine dressing

Quinoa is such a great grain to use in big chunky salads like this one. Although it's small, it has the capacity to carry, and is generous with it. Dressings love it, and once dressed it loves everything else. Here, tender roast squash, sweet onions and crunchy walnuts are all bound up in its spell. I like to finish this salad with a hint of Roquefort, one of my favourite blue-veined sheep's cheeses. But, of course, you could leave it out for a vegan version.

SERVES 6–8

150g (5½oz) quinoa, rinsed

1 teaspoon salt

1 squash, such as a butternut, halved, deseeded and cut into 5 or 6 wedges

2 red onions, halved and cut into wedges

1 garlic bulb, broken into cloves and peeled

2 tablespoons extra-virgin olive oil

2 teaspoons cumin seeds

2 rosemary sprigs, torn

75g (2½oz) walnut halves

1 large bunch of curly kale (about 150g/5½oz), stripped from the stalk

125g (4½oz) soft blue cheese, such as Roquefort (optional)

salt and freshly ground black pepper

FOR THE DRESSING

2 teaspoons wholegrain mustard

2 tablespoon extra-virgin olive oil

1 tablespoon sunflower oil

2 tablespoons red wine vinegar

1 tablespoon runny honey (or 2 tsp sugar as a vegan option)

1 garlic clove, peeled and bashed

Heat the oven to 200°C/400°F/gas mark 7.

First, make the dressing. Put all the ingredients in a small jug, season, and whisk until thoroughly combined. Set aside.

Put the quinoa in a large pan and cover with plenty of cold water – you'll need about three times as much water as quinoa. Add the salt, put over a medium–high heat and bring to the boil. Reduce the heat and simmer for about 10–12 minutes, or until the grains are tender. Drain well, then while the quinoa is still warm, spoon over half the dressing and turn it through the grains.

While the quinoa is cooking, scatter the squash, onions and garlic cloves out over a roasting tin. Trickle over the oil and sprinkle over the cumin seeds and rosemary. Season with salt and pepper and toss together. Roast for 45–50 minutes, turning occasionally or until everything is soft and caramelized.

Turn down the oven to 120°C/235°F/gas mark 1. Remove the roasting tin from the oven and add the walnut halves and kale. Use a spatula to turn the kale gently in some of the well-flavoured roasting oil. Return the tray to the oven and cook for a further 15–20 minutes, until the kale is crisp and the nuts are toasted.

At this stage remove the kale from the tin and set aside. Spoon the quinoa over the squash, nuts and onions and pour over the remaining dressing. Tumble everything together thoroughly, season to taste with more salt and pepper and spoon into a large bowl or out over a platter. Arrange the kale over the top of the salad and crumble over the cheese, if using. Serve straight away.

a kind of minestrone soup

Many of the things I ate as a child I have learned to cook from my memory – there wasn't anything written down. Soups, like this minestrone – which my mum made regularly and I absolutely loved – made such an impression on me that words, weights and measures were unnecessary. Instead, I can close my eyes and see her making it. I see the different vegetables and herbs, her dark oval chopping board and the heavy pan warming on the stove. I can see how it is built up, in layers, I can see the size of the little bubbles that rise to the surface as the soup simmers gently away. I remember the beans, the olive oil and the colour. But most importantly, the taste, texture and balance between the ingredients.

SERVES 6–8

3 tablespoons extra-virgin olive oil, plus extra to serve

1 large onion, chopped

3 or 4 carrots, peeled and cut into 4–5mm (¼in) cubes

4 tender celery sticks, sliced

4 garlic cloves, thinly sliced

3 or 4 bay leaves

2 x 400g (14oz) tins good-quality plum tomatoes

2 litres (70fl oz) vegetable stock

1 x 400g (14oz) tin of haricot beans, drained and rinsed

100g (3½oz) spaghetti

1 bunch of kale, chard or spinach, tougher stalks removed and leaves roughly chopped

a couple of handfuls of runner beans, stringy edges peeled and beans thinly sliced; or the same amount of green beans, topped and tailed and cut into pieces

1 small bunch of parsley, leaves picked and chopped

grated Parmesan, to serve

salt and freshly ground black pepper

Heat a large heavy-based pan over a medium heat and add the olive oil. When it's hot, add the onion, carrots, celery, garlic and bay. Season with salt and pepper. Cook gently, stirring regularly, until the vegetables begin to soften and smell sweet, about 10 minutes. Adjust the heat if you need to so that the vegetables don't colour.

Empty the tinned tomatoes into a bowl and use your hands to crush them thoroughly, then tip them into the pan with the soft vegetables. Cook, stirring occasionally, for 15–20 minutes, then add the vegetable stock and bring to a simmer. Allow the soup to cook gently for about 45 minutes, then add the haricot beans. Break the spaghetti into short lengths and add that, too. Return the pan to a simmer and cook for a further 30 minutes, then add the kale, chard or spinach and runner or green beans and stir well. Give the soup a final 15–20 minutes cooking, until all the vegetables are tender. If at any point it is looking too thick, add some water. Taste the soup and adjust the seasoning with salt and pepper, then stir in the parsley.

I like to take the pan off the heat and let the soup stand at this point, I think it benefits from 15–20 minutes just being, before you ladle it into bowls and serve trickled with plenty of your best olive oil and scattered with finely grated Parmesan cheese.

Don't worry if you don't eat it all in one sitting. This minestrone (and others like it) can taste even better the following day.

salad of chicory, chestnut mushrooms, kale & toasted seeds

This is one of my favourite raw salads. It's quick and interesting and has raw mushrooms in it (so underrated) – I'm a massive fan. Toasting mixed seeds in a splash of tamari makes them hopelessly irresistible and, if there are any left by the time you sit down, the perfect garnish to what is the perfect light lunch.

SERVES 2

2 tablespoons pumpkin seeds

2 tablespoons sunflower seeds

2 tablespoons tamari

2 small or 1 larger firm head of red chicory, leaves separated

about 100g (3½oz) very fresh, firm chestnut mushrooms

handful of very small, tender kale leaves, or chard if you can't find kale

FOR THE DRESSING

1 tablespoon extra-virgin olive oil

½ tablespoon red wine vinegar

1 teaspoon sugar

1 teaspoon Dijon mustard

salt and freshly ground black pepper

This is one of the simplest salads you could ever put together. Place a small pan over a low heat, add the seeds and tamari and cook, stirring regularly, until the seeds are toasted and the tamari has reduced to coat them, like a dry-roasted peanut – about 2–4 minutes. Remove from the heat and set aside.

Arrange the chicory leaves over a large plate. Slice the mushrooms and scatter these over the top of the chicory along with the kale or chard leaves and the toasted seeds.

To make the dressing, put all the ingredients in a small jug or bowl, season well with salt and pepper, and whisk well to combine. Trickle the dressing over the salad, season everything well with salt and pepper, and serve at once.

kohlrabi & dressed sprouted puy lentils

There are times when stripping something back to the bone is right. There are times when raw is more beautiful, and when two is greater than three. This salad is an example of that. It appears brutally simple, but this is not the case. Even bones have something inside them.

SERVES 2

100g (3½oz) dried puy lentils

2 small kohlrabi

lemon, for squeezing

FOR THE DRESSING

2 teaspoons sugar

2 teaspoons English or Dijon mustard

1 tablespoon cider vinegar

2 tablespoons extra-virgin olive oil

1 tablespoon sunflower oil

1 small garlic clove, peeled and bashed

½ lemon

salt and freshly ground black pepper

First, sprout your lentils. Place the dried lentils into a smallish glass bowl or jug and cover with plenty of cold water. Soak the lentils overnight, then drain and rinse. Return the seeds to the bowl and cover loosely with a square of clean cotton cloth. Leave the bowl somewhere cool and bright – the lentils don't need to be in the fridge.

After 24 hours, rinse the lentils in fresh cold water, drain and leave them for another 24 hours. Repeat this 24-hour, rinsing-and-leaving process once more. After the three days you'll notice that each lentil will have begun to sprout a little shoot. The lentils are ready to eat at this point.

To assemble the dish, first make the dressing. Put all the ingredients in a small jug or bowl, season well with salt and pepper, and whisk or stir really well to combine. Set aside while you prepare the kohlrabi.

Peel the kohlrabi, then use a very sharp knife or a mandoline to slice them around their equators, as thinly as you can.

Arrange the slices of kohlrabi equally over two plates. Squeeze over some lemon juice and season lightly with salt and pepper. Place a couple of handfuls of sprouted lentils in a bowl and trickle the dressing over liberally. Scatter the lentils over the kohlrabi, then season and serve.

roast pork & crackling with apples, fennel seed, sage, lemon & thyme

What are apples without pork? What is pork without crackling? What is a title if not a veneration of a recipe? How do we rate success? Perfect crackling, which is 'a thing', relies on the pork skin to be exceptionally dry. Take the pork out of its packaging as soon as you can, thoroughly dry the skin with kitchen paper or a clean tea towel, then leave it uncovered in the bottom of the fridge for at least 24 hours (48 hours would be better). Make sure the skin is scored properly, down through to the fat (of which there should be some) and salt it only as it goes in the oven, not before.

SERVES 6

about 2kg (4lb 8oz) pork loin, scored and tied

1 red onion, cut into 8–10 wedges

8 small apples, such as Cox's

2 lemons, sliced into 5mm (¼in) rounds

1 small bunch of sage, leaves picked

8 bay leaves

1 small bunch of thyme

handful of fennel fronds, if available

2 teaspoons fennel seeds, lightly bashed

2 tablespoons olive oil

salt and freshly ground black pepper

Heat the oven to 230°C/450°F/gas mark 9, or as hot as your oven will go. Place the pork (with its very dry skin – this is really important as we want it to crackle) on a suitably sized roasting tin. Season all over with salt, then place in the hot oven for 25–30 minutes. Once the crackling is looking good, remove the pork and turn the oven down to 190°C/375°F/gas mark 6½.

Scatter the red onion wedges over the base of a large, clean ovenproof dish. Carefully lift the pork from the hot roasting tin and set it down on top of the onions.

Place the whole apples around the pork, arrange the lemon slices in between them, scatter over the sage leaves, bay, thyme and fennel tops (if using) and season well with salt and pepper. Sprinkle over the crushed fennel seeds and trickle everything with the olive oil. Place the fragrant pork and apples in the oven and cook for a further 35 minutes, until the pork is cooked through and the apples are soft but not collapsing. (It's worth noting that if the apples look like they are going to collapse, you can take them out of the oven and allow the pork to finish cooking without them.)

Remove the pork dish from the oven and allow the meat to rest in a nice, warm place for 10–15 minutes. Serve everyone a few thick slices of pork, some generous strips of crackling, an apple and some lemony, herby juices.

potted shrimps

Potting is a very old way to preserve food. The process involves filling small bowls or crocks with warm meat or fish, then capping them with a layer of melted fat, which keeps out the air, and stops the contents spoiling. Before refrigeration, potting things was a necessity; now, it is more of a treat. Shrimps prepared this way have done what a lot of potted food has not – they have remained loved. Especially by me!

SERVES 4

175g (6oz) unsalted butter

zest of ½ lemon

2 good pinches of ground mace

2 good pinches of cayenne pepper

1 thyme sprig

200g (7oz) cooked and peeled brown shrimps

salt and freshly ground black pepper

Melt the butter in a pan over a low heat. Allow it to gently bubble, but not burn. As soon as you see the buttermilk browning, remove the butter from the heat and let it settle. Carefully pour the hot butter through a fine sieve into a jug or bowl, making sure you leave the buttermilk behind.

Clean the pan and pour in two-thirds of the melted butter. Add the lemon zest, mace, cayenne and thyme, along with a good pinch of salt and a generous twist of black pepper. Allow the butter gently to infuse over a low heat for 3–4 minutes, then remove the pan from the heat and add the shrimps, stirring them slowly into the butter.

After removing the thyme sprigs, divide the shrimps and butter equally between four ramekins or pots and place in the fridge to set. When the mixture is firm pour over the last of the melted butter to seal. Return to the fridge.

Remove the potted shrimps from the fridge 30 minutes or so before you intend to eat them. Serve on warm toast with a wedge of lemon for squeezing.

clams with tomato, pastis & parsley

How exquisite a thing is pastis; its clarity and its milkiness. It is the anise in the drink that lends itself to this dish so well. To the tomatoes it is an antidote; and to the shellfish, a drug. I like to serve these clams with a creamy polenta, which thanks to its nature, makes a perfect canvas. However, a buttery mash would work equally well. If you can't get hold of clams, then try this with mussels; it works in the same way.

SERVES 2

2 tablespoons olive oil

1 onion, halved and finely diced

2 garlic cloves, peeled and thinly sliced

finely grated zest of ½ lemon

1 teaspoon fennel seeds, crushed

2 bay leaves

1 rosemary sprig

1 x 400g (14oz) tin good-quality chopped tomatoes

½ teaspoon sugar

100ml (3½fl oz) pastis or Pernod

1kg (2lb 4oz) live clams, washed thoroughly (discard any with broken or open shells)

2–3 tablespoons chopped flat-leaf parsley

salt and freshly ground black pepper

Set a large, heavy-based pan over a medium–high heat. Add the olive oil and, when hot, add the onion and garlic. Season with a little salt and pepper and stir regularly, cooking for 6–8 minutes, until the onion is soft but not coloured.

Add the lemon zest, fennel seeds, bay and rosemary and continue to cook for another 2–3 minutes. Stir in the chopped tomatoes, then half fill the empty tin with water and pour in the water, too. Add the sugar, season with more salt and pepper, and bring to a gentle simmer. Cook for 20–25 minutes, stirring regularly, until the sauce is rich and thick.

Now, add the pastis or Pernod and turn up the heat. Once the liquid is boiling, add the washed clams, stir once, shake twice and place a close-fitting lid on the pan.

Cook for 3–4 minutes (shaking intermittently), or until all the clam shells are open. (Discard any clams that remain closed.) Remove the pan from the heat, stir in the chopped parsley and serve straight away.

mussels with parsley, white wine & sauté potatoes

I'd like a map on which to plot all the places I've sat and eaten mussels cooked like this. What shape would the waypoints make? This is a dish I never had to learn to love; I loved it the first time my mum made it for me and I've loved it every time it's been made (properly) for me since. When it's served with chips, it's called *moules-frites*, Belgium's national dish and something we see on menus throughout much of France. But I like to make my version with sauté potatoes instead. I find them less hassle than chips, and actually they're tastier.

SERVES 4

1 knob of butter

1 tablespoon olive oil

2 or 3 small shallots, diced

1 garlic clove, peeled and thinly sliced

½ glass of white wine

100ml (3½fl oz) double cream

2.5kg (5lb 8oz) large mussels, cleaned and debearded (discard any with broken or open shells)

small bunch of parsley, leaves picked and chopped

salt and freshly ground black pepper

FOR THE SAUTÉ POTATOES

500g (1lb 2oz) large white potatoes, peeled and cut into smallish bite-sized cubes

4 tablespoons olive oil, or a lighter oil

1 small bunch of oregano or marjoram, or 2 teaspoons dried

First, make the sauté potatoes. Place the potatoes in a large pan and cover with water. Salt the water, then place the pan over a medium–high heat. Bring the potatoes to the boil and cook, uncovered, until they are just tender, about 10–12 minutes. Drain the potatoes, gently roughing their edges with a little shake of the colander, and then leave them in the colander for the steam to evaporate. Heat a large heavy-based frying pan over a high heat. Add the oil, and when hot add the potatoes in a single layer (you may have to cook in batches). Scatter over the oregano or marjoram and season with salt and pepper. Use a spatula to turn the potatoes every so often, until they are golden and crisp on all sides, about 15–20 minutes. Line a dish with some kitchen paper, gently tip in the potatoes and keep them warm in a low oven.

To cook the mussels, heat the butter and olive oil in a large, heavy-based pan over a medium heat. When it's bubbling away, add the shallots and garlic, along with a pinch of salt and a good twist of black pepper. Cook the shallots, stirring regularly, for 4–5 minutes, until soft, but not coloured. Turn up the heat to high and add the wine and cream. As soon as the liquid comes to a rolling boil, throw in the mussels. Stir carefully, then immediately place a tight-fitting lid on the pan. Cook for 2–4 minutes, giving the pan a good shake every so often, until the mussel shells are all just open. Turn the parsley through the mussels and remove the pan from the heat. Discard any mussels that haven't opened up. Transfer the mussels and all their sauce to a large, shallow dish, scatter over the warm, crispy potatoes and bring the whole lot to the table.

tomato & anchovy tart with goat's cheese, marjoram & chilli

God, how I love this tart. It's rich, but with a kind of humble, peasant elegance I find extremely comforting. Oh! And it's incredibly moreish. Plus, it's so different from most pastry tarts I make, or eat. Its brilliance is thanks to a tomato-sauce filling – the sort you might serve with spaghetti. This is where the depth and the sweetness come from. It's just as delicious without the salted anchovies, but I can't help using them.

SERVES 4–6

2 tablespoons extra-virgin olive oil

1 onion, finely chopped

4 garlic cloves, peeled and very thinly sliced

½ teaspoon chilli flakes

3 bay leaves

2 x 400g (14oz) tins good-quality chopped tomatoes, or the equivalent weight in fresh

50g (1¾oz) Cheddar cheese, grated

150ml (5fl oz) double cream

2 eggs, whisked

1 small bunch of marjoram, chopped

200g (7oz) goat's cheese, cut into 1cm (½in) slices

12 anchovy fillets

salt and freshly ground black pepper

FOR THE SHORT CRUST

400g (14oz) plain flour

200g (7oz) butter, cubed and chilled

½ teaspoon salt

about 125ml (4fl oz) chilled water

First, make the short crust. Pulse the flour, butter and salt in a food processor until you have the consistency of breadcrumbs. With the motor running, steadily add the chilled water, stopping as soon as the dough comes together. Remove the dough, knead it a couple of times, then wrap it in cling film and chill it in the fridge for at least 30 minutes. Remove the pastry from the fridge and allow it to come up to room temperature. Heat the oven to 180°C/350°F/gas mark 6.

Roll out the dough to about 3mm (⅛in) thick. Line your tart case (I used a rectangular one, about 15cm x 25cm/6in x 10in) with the pastry, leaving an overhang. Prick the base, then line it with baking parchment and baking beans. Bake for 20 minutes, then remove the beans and paper and return to the oven for 10–12 minutes, until just golden. Remove from the oven and trim the overhang. Set aside.

To make the filling, set a medium heavy-based pan over a low heat. Trickle in the olive oil and, when it's hot, add the onion, garlic, chilli and bay leaves. Season, and let them sizzle for 6–8 minutes, stirring regularly, until the onion is soft but not coloured. Add the tomatoes and season lightly again. Cook, stirring regularly, for 35–40 minutes, until the sauce is thick and rich. Remove the pan from the heat and add the grated Cheddar and cream, followed by the eggs and half the chopped marjoram. Stir really well.

Heat the oven to 180°C/350°F/gas mark 6. Pour the filling into the pastry case and level it out. Arrange the goat's cheese slices over the filling, pressing them down a little. Scatter over the anchovies and remaining marjoram. Bake the tart for 35 minutes, or until set and a little blistered. Allow to cool for at least 25 minutes before serving.

2.25 P.M. | OCTOBER

Rosie's kitchen
Broadoak

a simple fermented cabbage recipe

When you salt cabbage and leave it in the right conditions something called lacto fermentation takes place. This happens because *Lactobacillus* – a naturally occurring bacteria that's on your hands right now, and on the vegetables in your fridge – feed on the sugars in the cabbage, producing lactic acid, which helps to preserve the cabbage. Fermented cabbage is very good for you because it contains lots of vitamins and fibre as well as probiotics – microorganisms that are great for your digestion and general gut health. It's important not to ignore these remarkable health benefits, but the main reason I like to ferment cabbage is for the flavour and texture, which are almost otherworldly.

MAKES 1 LARGE JAR

1 or 2 firm white or red cabbages (about 2.5–3kg/5lb 8oz–6lb 8oz), damaged or ragged outer leaves removed

40g (1½oz) salt

1–2 tablespoons caraway seeds

Before you begin, you'll need a 2-litre (70fl oz) scrupulously clean, sterilized jar with a lid and a plastic food bag.

Place the cabbage or cabbages on a large chopping board and cut into quarters. Remove the dense core, then use a large, sharp knife to slice the cabbage quarters across their width as thinly as possible. Place the shredded cabbage in a large plastic or metal bowl, sprinkle over the salt, and add the caraway.

Crush the cabbage through your hands repeatedly to break up the leaves and get the salt into it. It's hard work, but try and do this for 3–4 minutes. Cover the bowl and leave for an hour or so, then repeat the crushing process. The salt will have drawn a lot of liquid out of the cabbage. This liquid is called the brine. Pour the brine into the jar, then pack in the cabbage, pushing it down below the surface of the liquid. If there's not enough brine to cover the cabbage, simply mix 10g (¼oz) fine salt with 200ml (7fl oz) water and pour this over. Weigh down the cabbage using a clear plastic food bag part-filled with water, as in the photograph.

Leave the jar at an ambient temperature (16–22°C/60–72°F) with the lid left open for five to eight days. Taste the cabbage on the third or fourth day, and see how you like it. It should be sweet and not overly sour at this stage. I like to leave it to ferment for another two to four days before decanting into a large, clean, airtight plastic box. Store the cabbage in the fridge and eat within four to six weeks.

squash, chicory, hazelnuts & rosemary

Simple cooking is about understanding the balance of flavour and texture and how these components play out together on a plate. When you're using only three or four ingredients, there's nowhere to hide, so things really have to be there for a reason, or not at all. This wintry salad goes some way towards illustrating this point, and it does it in the most achievable and enjoyable of ways. I've used firm red chicory heads here, but you could use chunky wedges of radicchio, another of my favourite bitter-tasting leaves.

SERVES 4

4 tablespoons olive oil

1 onion, halved and thinly sliced

3 garlic cloves, peeled and sliced

750g (1lb 10oz) butternut squash, peeled and cut into 2–4cm (¾–1½in) cubes

150ml (5fl oz) vegetable stock

4 small heads of red chicory, halved

2 or 3 rosemary sprigs, roughly chopped

100g (3½oz) blanched hazelnuts

salt and freshly ground black pepper

First, make a butternut squash purée. Set a large heavy-based pan over a medium heat. Add 2 tablespoons of the olive oil to the pan, followed by the onion, two-thirds of the garlic, and all the squash. Season with a little salt and pepper. Gently fry, stirring regularly, for 10–12 minutes, then pour in the vegetable stock. Place a lid on the pan and cook for a further 15–20 minutes, or until the squash is tender.

Remove the pan from the heat and allow the contents to cool for 5–10 minutes. Spoon out the squash, onions and garlic into a jug blender, ensuring that you don't add too much liquid as you do so, as you want the purée to be nice and thick. Whiz the mixture until completely smooth. Season the purée to taste and set aside.

Set a large heavy griddle pan over a really high heat. When it's smoking hot, add the chicory heads, trickle with 1 tablespoon of the olive oil and season with salt and pepper. Griddle the chicory until it's charred on the outside and tender in the middle; 8–10 minutes on each side.

In a small pan, heat the remaining olive oil over a medium heat. Add the remaining garlic, the rosemary and the blanched hazelnuts. Fry gently for 3–4 minutes, until the garlic is soft, but not burned. Season with salt, remove from the heat and set aside.

To serve, spoon the purée out over a large, warm serving plate. Top with the chargrilled chicory and finish by scattering over the warm salty, garlicky hazelnuts.

3.30 P.M. | NOVEMBER

Mum's kitchen
Old Dairy House
North Eggardon

leek & potato soup with smoked cheese & chives

What is it that constitutes simple? I never know. In my experience even the simplest things can be complex. For example, take a small piece of driftwood that's been washed up on the beach. It's a fairly ordinary thing and plain enough to look at, but at one stage it was a part of a living tree; a plant that has evolved over millions of years, that feeds on sunlight, produces oxygen and is able to communicate with other plants through an intricate lattice of mycelium into which its roots connect. The simplicity of the naked form is skin deep. Underneath it is more complex and beautiful than we can possibly imagine.

SERVES 4

about 1 litre (35fl oz) vegetable (or chicken) stock

3 floury white potatoes (about 350g/12oz), peeled and cut into 1–2cm (½–¾in) cubes

3 medium–large leeks, trimmed and sliced into 1cm (½in) thick rounds

25g (1oz) butter

1 tablespoon olive oil

2 shallots or 1 onion, thinly sliced

2 garlic cloves, peeled and thinly sliced

2 or 3 thyme sprigs, leaves stripped

100ml (3½fl oz) double cream

50g (1¾oz) smoked Cheddar or goat's cheese, grated, plus extra for serving (optional)

1 small bunch of chives, finely chopped, plus a few left whole to serve (optional)

salt and freshly ground black pepper

Bring the stock to the boil in a large heavy-based pan. Add a third of the potato, bring the stock back to the simmer and cook, uncovered, for 6–8 minutes, or until the cubes of potato are just tender. Add a third of the leeks and cook for 3 minutes to soften, then drain the vegetables through a colander set over a large bowl to catch the stock. Return the pan to a medium heat. Add the butter and olive oil and, when bubbling, add the shallots or onion, the garlic and the thyme leaves. Cook, stirring regularly, for 4–5 minutes, then add the remaining leeks and potato to the pan and season well with salt and pepper. Cook gently, stirring regularly, for 3–4 minutes, then add the hot stock and bring the liquid to a gentle simmer.

Cook the soup for about 15 minutes, until the leeks and the potatoes are lovely and tender. Remove the pan from the heat and purée the soup until smooth and creamy. I find that a jug blender is the best tool for this job.

Return the soup to the pan. Add the cooked leeks and potatoes you prepared earlier, along with the cream, grated cheese and chopped chives. Season with salt and pepper, then put the pan back on the heat and bring gently back to a simmer. Stir well, remove from the heat, and allow to stand for 5 minutes before serving in bowls, seasoned with pepper and sprinkled with extra cheese and a few whole chives, if you like.

fermented cabbage, apple & celeriac salad with chia seeds & goat's cheese

I make this salad when I have a batch of fermented cabbage on the go (see page 170). I like the tang and the intensity you get from it. That said, you can make a very similar salad by simply shredding the cabbage and dressing it in cider vinegar, olive oil, a little soft brown sugar and some salt and pepper. Either way, sweet apples and earthy celeriac marry up perfectly here, thanks to their crunchy qualities. A flurry of chia seeds makes a characterful addition. These seeds are particularly full of omega-3s, vitamins and minerals, but if you can't find them you could try linseeds or hemp seeds instead.

SERVES 4

2 crunchy dessert apples, quartered, cored and thinly sliced

300g (10½oz) celeriac, peeled and cut into thin matchsticks

juice of 1 lemon

400g (14oz) red or white fermented cabbage (see page 170)

180g (6¼oz) goat's cheese, sliced into rounds (or crumbled if soft)

2 teaspoons chia seeds

salt and freshly ground black pepper

FOR THE DRESSING

2 teaspoons sugar

2 teaspoons English or Dijon mustard

1 tablespoon cider vinegar

2 tablespoons extra-virgin olive oil

1 tablespoon sunflower oil

1 small garlic clove, peeled and bashed

First, make the dressing. Put all the ingredients in a small jug or bowl, season well with salt and pepper, and whisk or stir really well to combine.

To make the salad, place the thin slices of apple in a large bowl and add the celeriac matchsticks. Pour over the lemon juice, season with salt and pepper and tumble everything together.

Scatter about three-quarters of the cabbage over a large serving platter. Trickle over a tablespoon or two of dressing, then arrange the apple and celeriac over the top. Arrange the goat's cheese evenly over the platter, followed by the remaining cabbage. Trickle over the remaining dressing and finish with a scattering of chia seeds and a final seasoning of salt and pepper.

smoked ham, cheese & parsley sauce toasts

Take everything that's good about ham and parsley sauce, put it on toast and grill it. That's what I thought, that's what I did, this is what happened. You don't have to use smoked ham, but it does go particularly well with the cheese (in this case, a rich, mature Cheddar).

SERVES 6

30g (1oz) unsalted butter

30g (1oz) plain flour

225ml (7¾fl oz) whole milk

50g (1¾oz) Cheddar cheese, grated, plus extra for grilling

2 teaspoons Dijon mustard

1 small bunch of chives, finely chopped

1 small bunch of parsley, leaves picked and chopped

6 thick slices of good-quality bread, lightly buttered on both sides

6 large slices of smoked ham

salt and freshly ground black pepper

Heat the grill to medium–hot.

Set a medium saucepan over medium heat. Add the butter and when it's bubbling away, add the flour and stir it in. Cook the flour for a minute or so, stirring regularly, then pour in the milk. Whisk the milk until it comes up to the boil and the sauce begins to thicken; about 3–4 minutes. Add the cheese, mustard, chives and parsley. Stir the sauce for a few minutes, until the cheese is melted and the sauce is nice and smooth. Season well with salt and pepper, then remove from the heat and set aside.

Lightly toast the buttered bread on both sides under the hot grill. Remove the grill pan from the grill and divide the ham equally between the six toasts. Spoon over the thick sauce and scatter over a handful of finely grated cheese. Place the tray back under the grill and cook until the sauce is bubbling and golden in places and the ham is piping hot. Serve straight away.

roast chicken, parsley & mustard pie

A roast chicken should always get a second chance – it deserves it. So, after you've finished eating (and while the chicken is still warm) take all the meat off the bone, then tear up the carcass and make a stock. The next day you'll have a small bowl of chicken and a jug of flavorsome stock in the fridge. The possibilities are infinite. The pie is the jewel in the leftover roast chicken's crown, and well worth the time it takes to make. I like to serve these individual pies warm with mashed potatoes and some buttered greens, but they are also good cold, with some pickles and a good cheese.

MAKES 2 INDIVIDUAL PIES
(OR 1 LARGE ONE)

50g (1¾oz) butter, plus extra for greasing

50g (1¾oz) plain flour

250ml (9fl oz) chicken stock

100ml (3½fl oz) double cream

1 small leek, sliced into 1cm (½in) thick rounds

about 200g (7oz) leftover roast chicken, torn into small chunks and shreds

small bunch of parsley, leaves picked and finely chopped

2 heaped teaspoons of wholegrain or Dijon mustard

20g (¾oz) Cheddar or Parmesan cheese

about 400g (14oz) short crust pastry (see page 122)

1 egg, beaten

salt and freshly ground black pepper

Heat the oven to 180°C/350°F/gas mark 6.

Set a large, heavy-based pan over a medium heat. Add the butter and when it's bubbling, stir in the flour. Cook for 1–2 minutes, stirring regularly. Pour in the chicken stock, stir well and bring to a simmer. Reduce the heat and allow to simmer for 3–4 minutes, then stir in the cream, followed by the leek, chicken, chopped parsley, mustard and cheese. Stir everything together over a low heat and season well with salt and pepper to taste.

To make two individual pies, grease two 400ml (14fl oz) pudding basins with butter. Roll out four discs of pastry, two of which are about 20cm (8in) wide, and two of which are about 15cm (6in) wide. Line the two pudding basins with the larger pieces of pastry, allowing 2–3cm (¾–1¼in) of overhang. Divide the filling equally between the two lined basins and level off. Brush the pastry rims with a little beaten egg, then carefully lay over the pastry lids. Use the tip of your finger to crimp the pastry lid to the base. Then take a sharp knife and trim off the overhang. Make a little slit in the top of each pie to allow the steam to escape as each cooks. Use the remaining beaten egg to brush the top of each pie, and place the pies into the hot oven for 45–50 minutes, until the tops are crisp and golden. Allow the pies to stand for 10–15 minutes before serving.

pork liver pâté with green peppercorns & sage

I think people get a little nervous about making pâtés and terrines. They think it's beyond their abilities or something. The truth is... it probably is. (I'm joking, it's not.) Rather, the truth is the majority of pâtés are really easy to put together, as long as you have a mincer. What's more, making your own pâté means you know exactly what's gone into it and where the meat has come from (something you can never really be sure of when you buy pâté from the supermarket or delicatessens). I use pork back fat in my pâté, which helps keep it beautifully moist, as well as streaky bacon offcuts. And I always seek out the freshest liver I can get hold of. Your butcher will be able to help you with all of these ingredients. Brined green peppercorns are characterful little things and liven up a pâté in a way I adore.

MAKES 1 LARGE TERRINE

300g (10½oz) very fresh pig's liver, cubed and tough ventricles removed

300g (10½oz) fatty pork belly, cubed

300g (10½oz) fatty bacon offcuts, cubed

1 small onion, chopped

2 garlic cloves, peeled and grated

2 tablespoons chopped sage

1 glass of red wine

75g (2½oz) fresh breadcrumbs

1 tablespoon green peppercorns in brine

150g (5½oz) pork back fat, cut into 3–4mm (⅛in) cubes

about 300g (10½oz) thinly sliced streaky bacon, to line the terrine

sea salt and freshly ground black pepper

Place the liver in a large bowl with the pork belly, bacon offcuts, onion, garlic and sage. Mix thoroughly, cover and refrigerate for 2–3 hours or overnight.

Set up your mincer fitted with the coarse plate (7–8mm/⅜in). Pass the meat and liver mixture through the mincer and put it back into the bowl. Add the wine, breadcrumbs, green peppercorns and pork back fat, and season with some salt and pepper. Mix well.

At this stage you can fry a little patty of the mixture, if you like, taste it and adjust the seasoning of the main mixture accordingly. Remember to compensate for the fact that this pâté will be served cold, which takes the edge off the seasoning.

Heat the oven to 120°C/235°F/gas mark 1. Line a 1-litre (35fl oz) terrine with cling film, leaving some overhang around the edges. Line the terrine with the bacon, leaving enough overhang to envelope the meaty mixture. Spoon in the pâté mixture and level off, then fold over the overhanging bacon, then the cling film. Cover with foil – or, if using a traditional terrine dish, use the heavy lids. Stand the terrine in a high-sided roasting tin and pour in enough hot water to come two-thirds up the sides of the terrine dish. Cook in the oven for 1½–2 hours. Check the core temperature of the pâté with a temperature probe; it should register no higher than 72°C/160°F. Remove the pâté from the oven and leave to cool completely. Refrigerate for 12–24 hours before serving.

warm salad of seared skirt steak, roast celeriac, red onions & herbs

Skirt steak is one of my favourite cuts of beef. It knocks the socks off fillet and sirloin and is relatively inexpensive by comparison. Skirt has a moist, open grain but needs careful cooking to really make it shine. You either cook it very gently for several hours until unctuous and giving, or sear it quickly on a very hot grill or in a pan and serve it pink. There is no middle ground. Here, I'm serving it with celeriac, roasted to a golden, nutty perfection alongside sweet red onions and crunchy seeds. I like to finish the salad with a couple of handfuls of fresh herbs, which lighten this gorgeous winter salad.

SERVES 4

1 celeriac (about 800g/1lb 12oz), peeled and cut into bite-sized chunks

2 red onions, halved and each half cut into 3 or 4 wedges

2 garlic cloves, peeled and sliced

2 rosemary sprigs, torn

1 small bunch of thyme, torn

2 bay leaves

2 tablespoons olive oil

15g (½oz) pumpkin seeds

15g (½oz) sunflower seeds

300g (10½oz) skirt steak

1 large handful of salad leaves and herbs

salt and freshly ground black pepper

FOR THE DRESSING

2 tablespoons extra-virgin olive oil

2 teaspoons Dijon mustard

2 teaspoons sugar

1 tablespoon red wine vinegar

Heat the oven 180°C/350°F/gas mark 6.

First, make the dressing. Put all the ingredients in a small bowl or jug, season with salt and pepper and whisk vigorously to combine. Set aside while you make the salad.

Scatter the celeriac over a large baking tray, then the onions, then the garlic, rosemary, thyme and bay. Trickle 1 tablespoon of the olive oil over and season well with salt and pepper.

Place the baking tray in the hot oven and roast, turning the celeriac occasionally, for 35 minutes. Remove the tray from the oven and scatter over the seeds, then return to the oven for a further 8–10 minutes, or until the celeriac is a little caramelized on the outside and tender in the middle. Remove from the oven and keep warm.

Season the steak all over with plenty of salt and pepper. Heat a medium–large frying pan over a high heat. Add the remaining olive oil and, when hot, add the steak. Cook for about 1–2 minutes on each side for rare; or 2–3 minutes on each side for medium. Lift the steak from the pan and keep warm.

Take a large, warmed serving platter and scatter over the roasted vegetables and seeds. Slice the skirt steak thickly across its grain and place this on and around the celeriac. Top with the salad leaves, then trickle over the dressing and bring to the table.

2.00 P.M. | JANUARY

Ines & Simon's
wonderful things
New House

crab with rhubarb, chilli, yoghurt & fennel seed

Crab is really good during the winter. The meat is rich and sweet and the shells are heavy with it. It's also a good time to pair it up with rhubarb, another seasonal ingredient you'll find in good shape throughout the colder months. Here, I roast the rhubarb gently, with a little sugar, chilli, olive oil and lemon zest until it's just about to give in. Roasting has to be gentle – if the oven's too hot, the rhubarb will cook too quickly and lose its shape. The crab is left pretty much unadulterated bar a little seasoning. Crunchy fennel seeds and natural yoghurt bring this cool, calm winter lunch together nicely.

SERVES 2

2–3 sticks of crisp, snappy rhubarb, cut into 4–5cm (1½–2in) pieces

zest and juice of 1 lemon

2 tablespoons unrefined golden caster sugar

½ medium–hot red chilli, deseeded and thinly sliced

1 tablespoon fennel seeds, toasted and lightly crushed

4 tablespoons extra-virgin olive oil

300ml (10½fl oz) thick Greek yoghurt

250g (9oz) white and brown crab meat, freshly picked from the crab (you want about 80 per cent white meat and 20 per cent brown)

salt and freshly ground black pepper

Heat the oven to 120°C/235°F/gas mark 1.

Place the rhubarb pieces in a medium, shallow baking dish and pour over the lemon juice. Sprinkle over the caster sugar, and scatter over the chilli and half the fennel seeds. Pour over 1 tablespoon of water and 1 tablespoon of the olive oil and tumble everything together.

Cover the dish tightly with a piece of foil and place it in the oven for 20–35 minutes, or until the rhubarb is soft, but not broken down. (How long this takes will depend on how thick the sticks of rhubarb are.) Remove the rhubarb from the oven and set aside to cool a little.

Divide the thick yoghurt between four plates or bowls, spreading it out over the base of each. Sprinkle over the remaining fennel seeds and the lemon zest, and season with plenty of salt and pepper.

Place the crab meat in a bowl, dress with 1 tablespoon of the olive oil and season with a little salt and pepper.

Arrange the dressed crab and the tender rhubarb over the yoghurt. Spoon over any sour–sweet cooking juices from the rhubarb baking dish and trickle over the remaining olive oil. Bring the plates or bowls to the table with some warm toast alongside.

buttered jacket potatoes with smoked trout, red onions, horseradish & chives

Buttered jackets celebrate the cooked potato in the simplest way. There's something almost magical about cutting through the crisp, puffed skin to the steaming, fluffy flesh inside. If you think about it, it's the first time that potato has ever seen the light, and it's already cooked. How different that is to all other potato preparations! Perhaps that's why baked potatoes taste so good – all that flavour is baked in. For this recipe, I bake whole red onions with their skins on, right next to the spuds. The same thing happens with the onions – all that wonderful sweetness is locked in and, once cooked, they taste amazing. If you can't find or make cold-smoked trout (page 76), you could use cold-smoked wild salmon or hot-smoked trout, instead.

SERVES 2

2 baking potatoes

2 large red onions, unpeeled

2 tablespoons soured cream, plus extra to serve

1 tablespoon creamed horseradish, plus extra to serve

1–2 tablespoons finely chopped chives, plus extra to serve

25g (1oz) butter

good-quality extra-virgin olive oil

200g (7oz) sliced smoked trout

salt and freshly ground black pepper

Heat the oven to 190°C/375°F/gas mark 6½. Wash the potatoes, then sprinkle them with a little fine salt. Place them on a baking tray with the whole onions. Put the baking tray in the middle of the oven and cook for 1–1¼ hours, or until both the potatoes and onions are cooked through. Remove the potatoes and onions from the oven, but leave the heat on.

Halve the cooked spuds and scoop out as much hot flesh as you can, without tearing the skins. Place the flesh in a bowl, then return the hollow skins to the oven for 10 minutes to crisp up. While the skins are crisping, mash the potato flesh with the back of a fork or a masher, if you like. Add the soured cream, horseradish, chives and butter, season with plenty of salt and pepper, and mix well.

When the skins have crisped up, remove them from the oven and spoon the potato filling back into them. Return the filled skins to the oven to warm through, about 8–10 minutes.

Use a sharp bread or serrated knife to halve the onions and remove the soft flesh. Discard the drier outsides. Season the onions with a little salt and pepper and a trickle of your best extra-virgin olive oil.

To serve, place two filled potato halves on each plate. Wedge in the soft roasted onions, arrange the smoked trout over the top and finish with a spoonful of extra soured cream, extra horseradish and a scattering of extra chives.

3.10 P.M. | FEBRUARY

Nan Duffy's
passing time
Innishfree

date, olive oil & fennel cake

If you like the peppery, herbaceous qualities of a good extra-virgin olive oil and the sweet, clean taste of fennel seed, then you're sure to like this cake, too. It's a dairy-free cake, so has a different feel from a classic sponge made with butter. It's denser, richer and full of that distinctive, gritty texture dates bring; they are extraordinary in this way. I like to make a quick syrup of honey and olive oil to trickle over the cake as it comes out of the oven, which the cake greedily soaks up the way a freshly baked focaccia soaks up sweet balsamic vinegar and grassy olive oil. This cake is amazing served warm with whipped mascarpone.

SERVES 8–12

250g (9oz) white self-raising flour

100g (3½oz) light soft brown sugar

150g (5½oz) unrefined golden caster sugar

pinch of salt

½ teaspoon baking powder

4 teaspoons fennel seeds, toasted and coarsely crushed

200g (7oz) soft sweet dates (medjool dates would be perfect), stoned

300ml (10½fl oz) extra-virgin olive oil, plus extra for greasing

zest and juice of 2 oranges

3 large eggs

4 tablespoons runny honey

Heat the oven to 165°C/320°F/gas mark 4½.

Place the flour, sugars, salt, baking powder and 2 teaspoons of the crushed fennel seeds into a large mixing bowl.

Place the dates, 250ml (9fl oz) of the olive oil and all the orange juice in the jug of a blender and whiz until you have a relatively smooth, fine mixture. Add the eggs and orange zest and whiz again to combine.

Pour the purée over the dry ingredients and, using a spatula, fold the two together thoroughly. You will have a sweet, fragrant batter.

Grease a 20cm (8in) springform cake tin, then line it with baking parchment. Spoon the mixture into the tin, spreading the cake batter evenly with the back of the spoon.

Place the cake in the centre of the oven and cook for 50–60 minutes, until a skewer inserted into the middle of the cake comes out clean. Avoid opening the oven to check the cake or the cake may sink a little. When the cake is ready, remove it from the oven and let it stand in the tin.

Warm the remaining olive oil together with the honey in a small pan over a medium heat. Use a cocktail or kebab stick to prick the surface of the cake all over. Spoon the hot honey and oil over the cake, allowing it to seep gradually into the warm sponge. Sprinkle over the remaining fennel seeds, then allow the cake to cool.

The cake will keep well for several days, but to my mind is best eaten while still warm.

steamed raspberry jam & rose-petal pudding

I can taste roses in raspberries, in the juice that pearls on their skin; it's like a perfume. When you cook raspberries for jam, sugar holds in their essence like you've made a perfume, it's so scented – a scent in a sugar prison. When you dry rose petals you trap their scent in a similar way, although it's still in the flower, and the flower is dead. How can something so dead be so alive? This pudding is a distillation of both raspberries and roses, and it works beautifully.

MAKES 1 LARGE PUDDING (SERVES 6)

100g (3½oz) unsalted butter, softened, plus extra butter for greasing

1 tablespoon dried rose petals (the small, red variety)

150g (5½oz) unrefined golden caster sugar

2 large eggs, plus 1 egg yolk

dash of vanilla extract, or the seeds from 1 vanilla pod

150g (5½oz) self-raising flour

pinch of salt

50g (1¾oz) fresh white breadcrumbs

5–6 heaped tablespoons raspberry jam

Begin by greasing a 1.5 litre (52fl oz) pudding basin with butter and scattering over the rose petals, trying to make sure some of them stick to the buttered sides as you do so.

To make the sponge, cream together the sugar and softened butter until pillowy, light and soft. Beat the eggs, the egg yolk and vanilla extract or seeds into the creamed butter mixture. Carefully fold in the flour, salt and breadcrumbs and combine to create the batter.

Spoon the raspberry jam into the prepared pudding basin, then spoon in the sponge batter. The batter should come two-thirds of the way up the basin. Cover the pudding with buttered baking parchment and tie a length of string around the rim of the basin to hold the paper in place.

Place an upturned saucer in a large pan and set the pudding on top. Pour in boiling water so that it comes halfway up the sides of the basin, then cover the pan, put it over a high heat and bring the water back to the boil. Reduce the heat and simmer the pudding for about 2 hours. Check the water level and top it up, if required.

After 2 hours, carefully remove the basin from the pan and allow it to stand for 15 minutes before turning it out onto a plate. Serve with plenty of double cream, ice cream, or custard.

NIGHT

Under the scar of the blue bough
Down among all the soft leaves
I find a hawk's feather

Holding it
I feel something's changed
The shape of the sea is different

The project I began is now so tender
I can see the bone
I put the feather with my spoons

That night I hear a war outside
It's just a fox crying you say
We eat as the candlelight crumbles away

crushed, crispy new potatoes with lemon & garlic

Freshly dug boiled new potatoes are one of the garden's great gifts. I like to serve them with plenty of salt and melted butter – divine! Sometimes, though, it's good to mix things up a bit, and this recipe does just that. The potatoes are boiled, but then they get crushed. Not mashed, not chopped, just lightly crushed so that their skins split and their soft insides break out. Then, they get roasted in a hot oven, with garlic, lemon zest and – when I can get hold of one – a bunch of fennel sticks. (You don't eat the fennel; it's just big on flavour.) The results, fennel or no fennel, are a joyous mix of the crisp and the soft and everything in between. These potatoes are great on their own with some beers and dips, or they make a superb side to a piece of grilled fish or a roast chicken.

SERVES 6

1kg (2lb 4oz) large new potatoes, scrubbed

4 tablespoons extra-virgin olive oil

1 handful of fennel sticks

pared zest of 1 lemon (in strips)

1 garlic bulb, cloves separated, skin left on

salt and freshly ground black pepper, plus extra salt flakes to serve

Heat the oven to 180°C/350°F/gas mark 6.

Place the potatoes in a large pan of salted water and bring to the boil over a high heat. Cook for about 12–25 minutes, until tender (cooking time will vary according to how fresh your potatoes are and the variety). Drain, then leave the potatoes in the colander for a few moments for the steam to evaporate. Tip out the cooked potatoes onto a board and give them bash with a heavy object. I use the base of the pan I cooked them in. Don't mash them though, just bash them into flatter shapes, exposing the flesh and maximizing their crisping potential.

Trickle half the olive oil into a large roasting tray. Distribute the potatoes evenly over the tray and wedge the fennel sticks in and around them. Scatter over the strips of lemon zest and the garlic cloves and season all over with salt and pepper. Trickle over the remaining oil and place the tray in the oven. Roast for 45–60 minutes, or until the spuds are super-crisp and crunchy.

Remove from the oven and sprinkle with a little more flaky salt before serving straight away.

nettles, butter & sheep's cheese gnocchi

This lovely, wintry supper is as much about the little baked potato and sheep's cheese gnocchi as it is about the stinging nettles and the rich, salty butter. They are equals, or partners in a delicious crime. Gnocchi take a little time to prepare, but they are worth the effort. In fact, every time I make them, I'm shocked I don't make them more. But if time is in question, you could serve the buttery tender nettles with pasta instead; a good pappardelle would be just right.

SERVES 4

500g (1lb 2oz) large Désirée potatoes, all roughly the same size, scrubbed

150g (5½oz) plain flour, plus extra for dusting

1 teaspoon fine salt

35g (1¼oz) hard sheep's cheese (such as pecorino), or Parmesan, finely grated, plus extra for serving

2 egg yolks

25g (1oz) butter

2 tablespoons extra-virgin olive oil

250g (9oz) nettle tops, tough lower stalks removed

salt and freshly ground black pepper

Heat the oven to 190°C/375°F/gas mark 6½. Bake the potatoes on the middle shelf of the oven for about 1 hour, until cooked through. Remove from the oven and, while the potatoes are still hot, halve them and spoon out the flesh into a sieve. Discard the skins.

To make the gnocchi, place the flour in a large mixing bowl, add the salt and grated cheese and lightly combine. Press the warm potato through the sieve into the bowl. Then, add the egg yolks and combine everything together with a light touch. If the dough seems too wet, add a shake more flour.

Tip out the gnocchi dough onto a floured surface. Shape it into a flattish rectangle, about 3cm (1¼in) thick, then use a knife to cut 3cm-wide (1¼in) lengths. Roll the lengths into sausages, each of about 1cm (½in) in diameter. Lay the sausages side by side, and cut them into 1.5cm-wide (⅝in) segments. Dust these with flour, and roll each over the tines of a fork, pressing your thumb into the back, so you have an indentation on one side and grooves on the other. Put the finished gnocchi on a flour-dusted baking tray.

When you're ready to cook the gnocchi, bring a large pan of salted water to the boil. Add the gnocchi and cook for about 2 minutes, or until they rise to the surface. Remove with a slotted spoon into a large, clean pan set over a low heat. Add the butter and olive oil.

Drop the nettles into the gnocchi boiling water and simmer for 2–3 minutes, until tender. Drain well – you might need to squeeze the nettles a little with the back of a spoon. Add the nettles to the pan of buttery gnocchi, season well, then toss everything together. Serve on warm plates with plenty more grated cheese and seasoning.

lamb's breast with white beans & samphire

Breast of lamb is an underrated cut. It's easy to get hold of, relatively inexpensive, packed with depth and flavour and embarrassingly easy to cook. It's the sort of fearless cut you can whack in the oven with some fresh rosemary and garlic cloves and forget about for hours. A low, gentle heat renders the rich fat, tenderizes the dark meat and crisps up the edges. What you'll find, in the base of the roasting tray, is something close to godliness, and for white beans there's nothing holier. I like to serve samphire with this dish because I think its delicate salinity and gentle crunch goes so well with lamb, but if it's not in season, try purple sprouting broccoli or a kale, instead.

SERVES 2 AS A MAIN

1 large lamb's breast (about 1kg/2lb 4oz) with some good fat and meat

1 tablespoon extra-virgin olive oil

4 garlic cloves, peeled

4 rosemary sprigs

1 small onion, thinly sliced

1 x 400g (14oz) tin haricot beans, drained

75g (2½oz) samphire

good squeeze of lemon juice

salt and freshly ground black pepper

Heat the oven to 220°C/425°F/gas mark 9. Place the lamb's breast in a roasting tin, season all over and rub in the olive oil. Roast for 20 minutes, then remove the tin from the oven, tuck the garlic cloves and three of the rosemary sprigs under the lamb, add a splash of water and cover loosely with baking parchment. Turn down the heat to 120°C/235°F/gas mark 1, place the tin back in the oven and cook the lamb for a further 2–3 hours, until very tender. Use tongs to lift the lamb's breast out of the tin onto a plate. Cover with foil and keep warm in a low oven. Reserve the tin and everything in it.

Set a medium heavy-based pan over a medium heat. Spoon in a little of the lamb's fat from the roasting tin and, when hot, add the sliced onion and remaining rosemary sprig. Cook, stirring regularly, for 12–15 minutes, or until the onion is soft, but not overly coloured.

Now add the drained beans and get them moving around the pan. Add 300ml (10½fl oz) of water to the reserved contents of the roasting tin and scratch and scrape at the caramelized sticky bits on the base. Tip all this flavour into the bean mixture and bring the liquid up to a simmer. Cook until the beans begin to break down and thicken, then season, remove from the heat and keep warm.

Bring a small pan of water to the boil. Add the samphire, and cook for 1–2 minutes, until the samphire is tender, then drain it and return it to the pan. Add the lemon juice and season with black pepper. To serve, place the lamb's breast onto a warm plate, spoon the creamy beans out alongside and scatter over the samphire.

5.50 P.M. | MARCH

Pamela Dixon
and sons'
Marine Parade

wood pigeon cured in apple with salt-baked beetroot & horseradish

The wood pigeon spends a life on the wing; its home is tracks of wood and open farmland. There are no chains in the skyway. There are no fences to keep the birds in or keepers to shut them up. They are wild and free and, as a result, benefit from a completely natural diet. What's more, they're very common, so their numbers will occasionally be culled. All this makes them one of the most sustainable and healthy forms of meat we could hope to eat. Beyond that... well, they are incredibly delicious.

SERVES 2 AS A STARTER

3–4 wood pigeon breasts

1 tablespoon extra-virgin olive oil

1 small knob of butter

horseradish sauce, to serve

pinch or two of beetroot powder (optional), to serve

salt and freshly ground black pepper

FOR THE BRINE

15g (½oz) salt

6 bay leaves

a few sprigs of thyme

2 garlic cloves, peeled and bashed

300ml (10½fl oz) apple juice

FOR THE BEETROOT

350g (12oz) fine salt

2 egg whites, lightly beaten

2 beetroot, scrubbed but not peeled

First, prepare the brine. Place all the brine ingredients in a medium pan over a medium heat. Bring to a simmer, then remove from the heat, transfer the liquid to a jug, cool, then put in the fridge to chill.

Once the brine is cold, place the pigeon breasts in a bowl and pour over the chilled brine. Place in the fridge for at least 12 hours, or overnight. Remove the pigeon from the brine and pat dry with kitchen paper, then pop in the fridge until you're ready to cook.

Next, prepare the beetroots. Heat the oven to 190°C/375°F/gas mark 6½. Combine the fine salt with the egg whites to make a thick paste. Mould equal amounts of the paste around each beetroot, then place them on a baking tray and bake for 1 hour, until tender.

To make the dish, set a medium frying pan over a high heat. Add the olive oil and when hot add the brined pigeon breasts. Fry the breasts for 2–3 minutes on each side, add the butter and baste the meat as it bubbles away. Cook for 1–2 minutes on each side, until the breasts are browned on the outsides and pink in the middle, then remove them to a plate and allow them to rest for 5 minutes in a warm place.

To serve, crack the salt crust away from the beetroot, slice each root in half and place two halves on each plate. Slice each pigeon breast in half (I like to do this on the diagonal), and divide equally between the plates. Add seasoning, a generous spoonful of horseradish sauce to each plate, and a sprinkling of beetroot powder, if using. Bring to the table and eat at once.

poached fish with seaweed, ginger & spring onions

This fragrant seaweed broth, gently spiced with garlic, chilli and ginger, would make a light, cleansing meal in its own right. But, I think, carefully poaching a piece of fresh, white fish in the broth, as it gently simmers away, turns the tables completely. Don't let the broth boil too hard, the most delicate of tremulous simmers is all that's required to cook the fish through. You can check that the fish is done by lifting a piece out with a fork to see whether the white flakes separate.

SERVES 2

5g (⅛oz) dried wakame seaweed

2 tablespoons sunflower seeds

3 tablespoons tamari or soy sauce

300ml (10½fl oz) fish stock

¼ small red chilli, deseeded and thinly sliced

a few slices of ginger root

1 garlic clove, bashed, skin on

4 small spring onions, thinly sliced on an angle

2 x 50g (2oz) white fish fillets (such as bass, bream or sole), skin on

salt

Soak the seaweed in cold water according to the packet instructions. It will grow in volume tenfold. When it's ready, drain and set aside.

Heat a small pan over a medium heat. Toss the sunflower seeds in 1 tablespoon of the tamari or soy sauce and add them to the pan. Toast until they are dry and fragrant, and are nutty in colour – about 2–4 minutes – then remove from the heat and set aside.

Pour the fish stock into a large pan, add the chilli, ginger and garlic and place over a medium heat. Bring to a simmer, reduce the heat to low and cook very gently for 10 minutes to allow the flavours to infuse.

Pour the stock through a sieve into a clean, small pan set over a medium heat. Add the soaked seaweed, the remaining tamari or soy sauce and the spring onions and bring to a simmer. Season the fish lightly with salt, then nestle each piece into the simmering broth, skin-side up. The liquid should just cover the fish. Poach the fish in the broth for 3–4 minutes, or until the fish is just cooked through.

Taste the broth and adjust the seasoning if you need to with more tamari or a little salt. Divide the fish and broth equally between two warm bowls, scatter over the toasted seeds and serve at once.

lobster with asparagus, tarragon, cream & sheep's cheese

How can I introduce you in the night, with your calcium on fire and all that.
How can I explain your season, a word for tarragon, or the feeling.

SERVES 4 AS A STARTER
OR 2 AS A MAIN

2 x 800g–1kg (1lb 12oz–2lb 4oz) live lobsters

30g (1oz) unsalted butter, softened

2 small shallots, halved and finely diced

1 garlic clove, peeled and grated

pinch of chilli flakes

125ml (4fl oz) double cream

2 tablespoons chopped tarragon, plus extra for sprinkling

1 teaspoon Dijon mustard

12 asparagus spears

1 handful of white breadcrumbs

25g (1oz) hard sheep's cheese (such as pecorino), or Parmesan, finely grated

extra-virgin olive oil

2 or 3 thyme sprigs, leaves picked

salt and freshly ground black pepper

Prepare your lobsters for cooking by putting them in the freezer for about 35–40 minutes. This puts them to sleep and is far more humane than dropping them directly into boiling water.

Meanwhile, place a large frying pan over a medium heat. Add the butter and, when bubbling, add the shallots, garlic and chilli. Season, then cook, stirring regularly, for 8–10 minutes or until the shallots are soft, but not coloured. Add the cream, tarragon and mustard and 2–3 tablespoons of water. Bring the liquid up to a gentle simmer, then take the pan off the heat, season again to taste, and set aside.

Bring a very large pan of salted water to a rolling boil. Add the asparagus and cook for 1–2 minutes, then remove with a slotted spoon and set aside. Remove the lobsters from the freezer and drop them into the same water. Cook for about 1 minute for every 100g (3½oz); about 8–10 minutes. Once cooked, remove and allow to cool.

Put one lobster on a board with the head towards you. Place the tip of a sharp, heavy knife on the cross at the top of the head. Press down, cutting through the head, and pull the knife towards your body. Turn the lobster around so that the tail is facing you. Cut from the split in the head down through to the tip of the tail in one, firm motion, keeping your blade central. Repeat with the second lobster.

Heat the grill to medium. Remove the tail and claw meat, roughly chop it and add it to the warm cream along with the asparagus spears. Tumble everything together, taste, and season if you need to.

Pile the lobster, asparagus and tarragon cream back into the lobster shells. Combine the breadcrumbs with the cheese and a trickle of olive oil. Sprinkle the mixture over the filled lobster, scatter over the thyme and a little extra tarragon and place under the grill for 3–4 minutes, or until golden and bubbling. Serve with a salad dressed with lemon and olive oil.

ceviche with rhubarb, lemon & chilli

Ceviche is made by marinating very fresh fish in the juice of lemon, orange or lime. The acidity in the juice tenderizes the fish, and if you leave it long enough appears to cook it. The preparation has its origins in Peru, but you'll find thousands of interpretations of the same principle throughout much of South America. My approach has always been one of 'less is more' – I like the purity of a ceviche, so I tend to keep it as refined as I can. Here, I'm using the juicy pulp from grated rhubarb, alongside a little lemon to dress the fish. It's different from the more traditional way of doing things, but the results are just as good. Thinly sliced rhubarb gives the dish a real hit of texture and red chilli brings the fire.

SERVES 4

1 very fresh black bream or wild sea bass (about 800g/1lb 12oz), filleted, skinned and pin boned

1 stick of firm, red rhubarb, trimmed top and bottom

juice of 1 lemon and zest of ½

2 teaspoons caster sugar

1 red chilli, halved, deseeded and very thinly sliced

salt and freshly ground black pepper

Place the fish on a board and use your sharpest knife to cut 3–4mm-thick (⅛–¼in) slices across the fillet at a slight angle. Place these in a medium bowl. Don't add any fish flesh that appears tough or sinuous.

Weigh out 30–40g (1–1½oz) of the rhubarb and grate it very finely (I find a microplane is best for this task). Add the grated rhubarb pulp to the bowl with the fish. Then, cut the remaining rhubarb into slices no thicker than about 3mm (⅛in). Add the sliced rhubarb to the fish, along with the lemon juice and zest, and the sugar, chilli, plenty of salt to season and a twist of black pepper. Tumble the fish through all the ingredients – do this carefully, as you don't want to break it up. Taste and adjust the seasoning if you need to.

Divide the fish and rhubarb mixture equally over four plates or bowls. Spoon over any remaining sharp, sweet juices and serve straight away.

roast artichokes with garlic, sage, hazelnuts & lemon & fennel mayo

Sitting down to a plate of globe artichokes is more an experience than a meal. It's all fingers, butter, chins and smiles. To eat, work through the outer artichoke leaves first – pull them off, dip them in the lemony mayonnaise, then use your teeth to scrape the delicate flesh from the base. When you reach the hearts, squeeze some of the roast garlic out over some good bread or toast, top with a generous spoonful of the mayonnaise, followed by a few cracked hazelnuts. Finally, top with slices of the soft, buttery heart. It's delicious.

SERVES 4

4 large, heavy globe artichokes

6–8 small-to-medium wet or green garlic bulbs, tops trimmed

25g (1oz) butter

50g (2oz) hazelnuts, lightly bashed

1 generous handful of small sage leaves

4 tablespoons extra-virgin olive oil

salt and freshly ground black pepper

FOR THE MAYONNAISE

½ small garlic clove, peeled and grated

2 large egg yolks

½ teaspoon English mustard

juice and finely grated zest of 1 small lemon

½ teaspoon toasted fennel seeds, ground

175ml (5½fl oz) sunflower oil

75ml (2¼fl oz) extra-virgin olive oil

1 small bunch of fennel tops, chopped

First, make the mayonnaise. Place the garlic, egg yolks, mustard, lemon juice and zest and fennel seeds in a food processor. Season and whiz for 30 seconds. Combine the oils in a jug. With the processor running, slowly add them to the mixture, a few drops at a time at first, then in a trickle. Once you've added all the oil, you should have a thick, glossy mayo that holds its shape. Stir in the chopped fennel tops, taste and add more salt, pepper, mustard or lemon, if required. If the mayo seems too thick, stir in 1–2 tablespoons of warm water. Set aside

Bring a large saucepan of salted water to the boil. Add the artichokes (in batches, if necessary) and bring back to a simmer. Simmer for 15–40 minutes (depending on size and freshness) with the lid on, until the bases of the artichokes take the point of a knife. Lift from the water and set aside to cool. Add the garlic bulbs to the same boiling water and bring back to a simmer. Cook for 15 minutes. Remove the garlic and allow to cool a little, too.

Preheat the oven to 200°C/400°F/gas mark 7. Use a large knife to cut each artichoke in half from top to bottom. Use a teaspoon to remove the hairy chokes from the centres and remove any bigger, loose leaves from around the outside. Arrange the hearts and the garlic bulbs over a large roasting tray. Place a little butter inside each artichoke half. Scatter over the hazelnuts and sage leaves. Trickle the olive oil over everything and season well.

Place the tray in the oven and roast, turning everything once or twice, for 30–35 minutes. Remove the tray from the oven and bring to the table with the mayonnaise and some good bread.

roast tomatoes with potato purée & grilled bread

The English fry-up inspired this dish, but forget the bacon and sausages for a moment – this version is about the fried tomato, the toast and the potato cake. It might be just me, but that mouthful of juicy, sweet tomato, crunchy oily toast and soft, rich potato is such a good part of the breakfast that I felt it needed its own stage on which to be so amazing. It turned out to be a big show... massive, in fact. So much goodness, so much comfort and so much texture, you'll want to make it again and again.

SERVES 2–4

1kg (2lb 4oz) mixed, ripe tomatoes, larger ones halved

1 handful of mixed herbs, such as rosemary, thyme, lovage and basil, leaves picked and torn as necessary

150ml (5fl oz) good-quality extra-virgin olive oil, plus extra for the toast

500g (1lb 2 oz) floury white potatoes, such as King Edward or Maris Piper

4 garlic cloves

4 bay leaves

6–8 slices of sourdough or country bread

salt and freshly ground black pepper

Heat the oven to 150°C/300°F/gas mark 3.

Place the tomatoes in a large roasting tin, cut-side up, as necessary. Scatter over the herbs, then trickle everything with 2 tablespoons of the olive oil. Season the tomatoes really well with salt and pepper. Place the tray in the oven and roast for about 1 hour, until the tomatoes are soft and blistered and lovely.

While the tomatoes are roasting, cut the peeled potatoes into equally sized pieces, each no smaller than a golf ball. Place them in a large pan and cover with cold water. Set the pan over a high heat, add the garlic cloves, bay leaves and 3–4 teaspoons of salt. Bring the liquid to the boil and cook the potatoes for 20–30 minutes, or until they are nice and tender.

Drain the potatoes, discarding the bay leaves and the garlic cloves but reserving about a cup of the cooking liquid. Return the drained potatoes to the pan and leave them for 5 minutes to allow the steam to evaporate.

Mash the potatoes. After the first minute or so of mashing, gradually add the reserved cooking liquid along with the remaining olive oil. Continue to mash until the potato is smooth, light and well combined with no lumps. It shouldn't be stiff – it should be more of a purée. Season with salt and pepper and set aside to keep warm.

Toast, grill or chargrill the bread, trickle it with a little olive oil and set aside. To serve, spoon the potato purée out over a large, warm serving platter. Lift the tomatoes from their roasting tin and place them all over the top of the potato. Spoon over all the roasting juices and herbs and serve with the toast.

chicken livers with new potatoes, ricotta & sage

I love this rustic, hearty supper dish. It's an unpretentious pairing of very affordable ingredients that come together in such a natural, effortless way. Perhaps that's what makes it feel so Italian; or perhaps it's just the ricotta cheese I use. Look for fresh, free-range or organic chicken livers; they will make all the difference here. You can make the same dish in the winter with larger, main-crop potatoes, too.

SERVES 2

200g (7oz) small–medium new potatoes, scrubbed and cut into large bite-sized chunks

4 tablespoons extra-virgin olive oil

1 large red onion, thinly sliced

200g (7oz) chicken livers, trimmed

1 handful of small sage leaves (about 12–16 leaves)

1 small knob of butter

2 garlic cloves, peeled and thinly sliced

180g (6¼oz) ricotta cheese

salt and freshly ground black pepper

Place the potato chunks in a large pan. Cover generously with cold water and set over a high heat. Add 2 teaspoons of salt and bring the water to the boil. Cook the potatoes for 8–15 minutes (cooking time will vary according to how fresh your potatoes are and the variety), until tender.

Set a large frying pan over a high heat. Add half the olive oil and, when hot, add the red onion and the cooked new potatoes. Season with salt and pepper and fry, turning regularly, for 12–15 minutes, or until the potatoes have taken on some colour and are crisping around the edges. Remove the potatoes and onion from the pan and set aside to keep warm. Set the same pan over a high heat. Add the remaining olive oil and when it's super-hot, add the chicken livers and sage. Season them well with salt and pepper and cook them for 1–2 minutes on each side, then, when you're happy with their doneness, drop in the butter and garlic, and toss them about in the pan for a further 10–20 seconds, then remove from the heat.

Spread the ricotta evenly over the base of one large or two smaller plates. Spoon over the warm fried potatoes and onion, and finish by arranging the hot livers and sage leaves over the top. Spoon over any buttery juices you have left in the pan and bring to the table. Serve with good bread and a green salad.

8.30 P.M. | JULY

Polly's gran's
night sailing
Lyme Regis

spaghetti with tomato & fried chicken

Everyone who eats this dish falls in love with it immediately. Then, they go away and make it for themselves or for their family or friends. That's what good food does, that's what it is. This is not my dish, though, it was my mum's. Now I cook it, Alice cooks it, my brother cooks it, even my daughters cook it. I'm not sure exactly what makes it so, so good, but I can't implore you enough to try it, because I genuinely know you'll love it as much as I do. And, when you do, we will have created something that lives forever.

SERVES 2

2–3 tablespoons extra-virgin olive oil

1 onion, finely chopped

2 garlic cloves, peeled and thinly sliced

pinch of chilli flakes (optional)

1 rosemary sprig

2 or 3 bay leaves

500g (1lb 2oz) skinned, ripe tomatoes, chopped; or 1 x 400g (14oz) tin good-quality chopped tomatoes

1 teaspoon sugar

2 chicken breasts (each about 200g/7oz)

3 tablespoons plain flour

1 egg, beaten

100g (3½oz) white breadcrumbs

2 tablespoons light oil (such as sunflower)

2 or 3 thyme sprigs

about 100g (3½oz) spaghetti

1 knob of butter

grated Parmesan, to serve

salt and freshly ground black pepper

Place a heavy-based pan over a medium heat. Add the olive oil, followed by the onion, garlic, chilli, rosemary and bay leaves. Season with a little salt and pepper and cook gently, stirring occasionally, for 8–10 minutes, until the onion is soft but not coloured. Add the chopped tomatoes, sugar and a good splash of water. Place a lid on the pan and simmer for 35–40 minutes, until the tomatoes are breaking down and tender. Remove the lid and cook for a further 8–10 minutes to thicken the sauce. Taste, adjust the seasoning, remove from the heat and keep warm.

While the sauce is cooking, prepare the chicken. Slice each breast in half as evenly as you can across its face, giving you four much thinner, similar-sized pieces. You can tap them out using a rolling pin to get them nice and thin. Season them with salt and pepper, then toss them in the flour, dip them in the egg and finally cover them liberally with the breadcrumbs.

Heat a large, heavy frying pan over a medium–high heat. Add the light oil and, when hot, add the breaded chicken and the thyme sprigs. Fry for 6–8 minutes on each side, or until the chicken is cooked through and the crumb is crisp and golden.

Cook the spaghetti in a large pan of salted water until done to your liking. Drain, then return the pasta to the pan. Add the tomato sauce, the butter and a little more seasoning and stir everything through carefully. Divide the spaghetti between two warm plates, sprinkle with a little Parmesan and serve on the plate alongside equal portions of the fried chicken.

chicken liver pâté

Around Christmas time I always make a chicken liver parfait. It's completely divine, and so worth making if you have the time, but it is involved – there are eggs, there are reductions, there are bain-maries and there are deeply disappointing repercussions should it overcook. This version, on the other hand, couldn't be easier or more delicious and, provided you have some lovely chicken livers to hand, comes together in minutes instead of hours. I love it spread on toast with something sharp to cut its richness, like my pickled cucumbers (page 116), or with something sweet, like a spoonful of my blackcurrant jam (page 32).

SERVES 6–8

300g (10½oz) very fresh free-range or organic chicken livers

2 or 3 thyme sprigs, leaves stripped

125g (4½oz) unsalted butter

1 large or 2 smaller shallots, finely diced

1 garlic clove, peeled and crushed

3 tablespoons port

50ml (2fl oz) double cream

salt and freshly ground black pepper

Use a sharp knife to trim away any connective tissue or sinew from the livers. They should look smooth, plump and red. Season the trimmed livers all over with salt and pepper and sprinkle over the thyme leaves.

Set a medium heavy-based frying pan over a medium heat. Add 20g (¾oz) of the butter and, when it's hot and bubbling, add the shallots and garlic. Fry, stirring regularly, for 6–8 minutes until the shallots are soft but not coloured. Turn up the heat to high and add the seasoned livers. Fry for 30 seconds on the first side, flip them, and do the same on the second. Add the port to the pan and allow it to bubble and quickly reduce by two-thirds.

Add the cream to the pan and once it begins to bubble and thicken, tip everything into a blender and purée until smooth. With the motor running, slowly add the remaining butter in small chunks. The heat of the livers will melt the butter and it will emulsify into the other ingredients. Season the mixture well with salt and pepper, then pass it through a fine sieve into a clean bowl. You may need to use the back of a spoon to help it through.

Transfer the mixture to a bowl or, if you like, individual ramekins and place in the fridge for at least 2 hours to set.

Take the pâté out of the fridge 30 minutes before you intend to serve it. Spread it thickly on warm toast, season if you like, and serve as it comes, or with pickled cucumbers or blackberry jam.

celeriac, plum & blackberry salad

Take up the roots, all the briar fruit. Wipe the ash from the plums. Cut away the frail comb, the garden herbs.
I'm sorry we give nothing back, I'm sorry.

We owe this striking autumnal salad to the Earth, every single element comes from the dark soil around us. It makes you wonder how we repay her for that.

SERVES 4–6

1 firm celeriac (about 1kg/ 2lb 4oz), peeled and cut into 3–4cm (1¼–1½in) chunks

3 tablespoons extra-virgin olive oil

500g (1lb 2oz) ripe plums, halved and stoned

1 small handful of sage leaves

a few sprigs of rosemary

100g (3½oz) blackberries

runny honey, to taste

salt and freshly ground black pepper

Heat the oven to 180°C/350°F/gas mark 6.

Place the celeriac chunks in a baking tray, season with salt and pepper and sprinkle over 2 tablespoons of the olive oil, making sure the celeriac is nicely coated. Place the celeriac in the oven and roast for about 30 minutes, then remove the tray from the oven and carefully arrange the plum halves in and around the chunks. Tuck in the sage and rosemary, and trickle everything with the remaining olive oil. Return the tray to the oven, and continue roasting for 15–20 minutes, until the plums are lovely and soft, but still holding a little shape. Keep your eye on them as plums can cook at different rates depending on how ripe they are.

When you're happy with how everything is looking, remove the tray from the oven and scatter over the blackberries. Taste the celeriac and plums, seasoning with salt and black pepper, and trickling over a little honey to sweeten, if necessary.

Transfer the salad to a bowl or platter and serve straight away.

baked celeriac

This is a brilliant, fuss-free way to cook a whole celeriac. You don't even need to peel it – just place it in the oven for a couple of hours. During this time the flesh within will soften beautifully while retaining all its moisture, flavour and earthy, nutty character. I like to slice it open at the table, and season it then and there. It'll be crying out for butter, extra-virgin olive oil, salt and pepper, so don't hold back. I've sprinkled seaweed salt over this one. It's widely available and complements the celeriac beautifully. Isn't it lovely how such a humble vegetable can make such a spectacle, without even trying?

SERVES 2–4

1 large celeriac (about 750g–1kg/1lb 10oz–2lb 4oz)

2 tablespoons extra-virgin olive oil

50g (2oz) butter

seaweed salt and freshly ground black pepper

Heat the oven to 190°C/375°F/gas mark 6½.

Scrub the celeriac, but don't peel it. Put the whole celeriac on a baking tray and place it in the oven for about 2 hours, until the centre of the celeriac takes the point of a knife with ease.

Cut the celeriac in half and use a sharp knife and a fork to mash and chop the tender flesh. Once you've broken up the flesh a bit, add the oil and butter and continue to mash it in really well.

Season the celeriac all over with the seaweed salt and black pepper and serve at once.

235

roast cauliflower with buckwheat, thyme & truffle oil

This charming dish makes the most of the humble cauliflower. The contrast between the roasted florets, with their light crunch and bitter edge, is balanced perfectly by the sweet, velvety smooth purée underneath, which I embellish with a spoonful of good truffle oil. Toasted buckwheat, something I've always been really fond of, brings yet more crunch and character. This recipe makes a lovely starter or an equally lovely accompaniment to roast lamb or some grilled steak.

SERVES 2

1 cauliflower (about 500g/ 1lb 2oz), trimmed and broken into florets

2 tablespoons extra-virgin olive oil

3–4 thyme sprigs

2 tablespoons buckwheat groats

25g (1oz) butter

½ small onion, sliced

2 garlic cloves, peeled and sliced

about 200ml (7fl oz) chicken stock (or vegetable stock)

2 tablespoons best-quality truffle oil

salt and freshly ground black pepper

Heat the oven to 200°C/400°F/gas mark 7.

Scatter half the florets out over a medium roasting tray. Trickle over half the olive oil and season well with salt and pepper. Scatter over the thyme sprigs, then place the whole tray in the hot oven for 15–20 minutes, or until the cauliflower is tender and charred round the edges. Remove from the oven and set aside to keep warm.

While the cauliflower is roasting, toast the buckwheat. Scatter it out over a small baking tray and place it in the oven for 6–8 minutes. Remove and set aside to allow to cool.

Place a medium pan over a low–medium heat. Add half the butter and the remaining olive oil and, when bubbling, add the sliced onion and garlic. Cook gently for 5–6 minutes, or until the onion is soft and beginning to caramelize a little. Add the remaining cauliflower florets and season with a little salt and pepper. Pour over the chicken stock and place a lid on the pan. Bring the stock to a simmer and allow to bubble away gently for 6–8 minutes, or until the cauliflower is tender. Drain the cauliflower, reserving a little of the cooking stock, and put the florets into a jug blender with the remaining butter. Whiz to a smooth purée consistency, adding some of the reserved stock if necessary. Stir in half the truffle oil and adjust the seasoning to taste.

To serve, spread the warm purée over a warm serving plate or platter. Scatter over the roasted cauliflower florets and thyme sprigs, add a sprinkling of crispy buckwheat and finish with the remaining truffle oil. Serve at once.

roasted roots, fennel & squash with labneh

Labneh is a Greek yoghurt cheese made by salting and straining natural yoghurt until it is thick and creamy. You can buy it in good delicatessens, but it's so easy to make at home, I wouldn't bother. Labneh is usually made from cow's milk yoghurt, but I love the flavour of this sheep's yoghurt version even more, especially with a warm salad, like this one.

SERVES 4

1 onion squash or butternut squash (about 1–1.5kg/ 2lb 4oz–3lb 5oz)

4 small beetroot (each about golf-ball size)

½ celeriac

1 fennel bulb, with fronds (fronds optional)

2 red onions

1 garlic bulb, cloves separated but skin left on

4–5 thyme sprigs

4–5 rosemary sprigs

2 teaspoons fennel seeds

about 4 tablespoons extra-virgin olive oil, plus extra to serve

½ lemon, for squeezing

salt and freshly ground black pepper

FOR THE LABNEH

500ml (17fl oz) plain, whole sheep's or cow's yoghurt

1 teaspoon fine sea salt

First, make the labneh. You'll need to do this 6–8 hours before you want to eat the dish, but you can even start it several days in advance. Place the yoghurt in a bowl, add the salt and stir it in. Line a large sieve with muslin or cheesecloth. Spoon the salted yoghurt into the cloth, then gather up the sides and tie at the top. I like to suspend the yoghurt pouch over a bowl to drain, but you can leave it sitting in its sieve over a bowl. Transfer to the fridge and leave for 6–8 hours, or longer. When a significant amount of liquid has drained into the bowl and the yoghurt has the texture of thick crème fraîche or clotted cream, transfer the labneh into a clean bowl, cover and refrigerate. Pour off any further liquid before serving.

To prepare the dish, heat the oven to 180°C/350°F/gas mark 6. Halve and deseed the squash. Cut each half into 3–4cm (1¼–1½in) wedges. Arrange the wedges in a large roasting tin. Scrub and halve the beetroots. Peel the celeriac and cut it into 3–4cm (1¼–1½in) pieces. Trim the fennel, reserving any green fronds. Remove the outer leaves, then halve the bulb, and cut each half into three or four wedges. Peel the onions and cut them into wedges, root to tip. Add the vegetables to the tin with the squash, along with the garlic, thyme, rosemary, fennel seeds, and the reserved fennel fronds. Season well, trickle everything with olive oil and toss together.

Roast the veg for 30 minutes, gently stir and then roast for 15–20 minutes more, or until everything is tender and beginning to colour. Remove from the oven, stir again and cool for 15–20 minutes.

To serve, spoon a thick layer of labneh over the base of a large bowl or serving platter. Heap the warm vegetables, herbs and all the roasting juices on top of the labneh, squeeze over the lemon juice, and finish with a trickle more olive oil and some salt and pepper.

creamed spinach

When I was younger we used to take the occasional summer holiday in southern France. I remember the long, hot drive, in the old Citroen CX. My brother, sister and I would all go to sleep in the boot. We'd stay in our dear friend Peter's house, just south of Cahors. The food was simple there – bread, cheese, saucisson, some duck cooked on the fire, lentils and such. It was on one of these trips that I first tasted creamed spinach. We'd stopped at Le Moulin de l'Abbaye in Brantôme. I'd never eaten anything quite like it before; it made me so happy I was allowed to order another serving.

SERVES 2

300ml (10½fl oz) whole milk

½ onion, thinly sliced

1 garlic clove, bashed, skin on

2 bay leaves, torn

500g (1lb 2oz) main crop spinach

50g (2oz) butter, plus extra for finishing

40g (1½oz) plain flour

nutmeg, for grating

1 large handful of white breadcrumbs (keep them coarse)

1 large handful of finely grated Cheddar cheese

salt and freshly ground black pepper

Heat the oven to 180°C/350°F/gas mark 6.

Pour the milk into a medium pan and place it over a medium–high heat. Add the onion, bashed garlic and bay leaves and bring the mixture to a gentle simmer. Remove the pan from the heat and allow the flavours to infuse the milk for 15–20 minutes.

Meanwhile, bring a large pan of water to the boil. Drop in the spinach and cook for 1–2 minutes, until the leaves are tender. Drain, and when cool enough to handle, squeeze all the excess liquid from the spinach. Roughly chop it, and set aside.

Now make a white sauce. Set a medium pan over a medium heat, add the butter and, when bubbling, add the flour. Stir and cook for 1 minute, then pour in the infused milk, straining it through a sieve as you do so. Discard the onion and herbs. Use a whisk to work the white sauce as you cook it for 1–2 minutes, until it thickens. Season well with salt and pepper and a good grating of nutmeg, then turn off the heat and fold in the chopped, cooked spinach. Spoon the creamy spinach into a small ovenproof dish.

Combine the breadcrumbs with the cheese and scatter this over the surface of the spinach mixture. Dot with a little butter and place in the oven for 8–12 minutes, or until crisp and golden on top and bubbling hot underneath. Serve at once.

onion soup, grilled cheddar toasts & fried apples

A rich onion soup is a bowl of hope. When we're tense or tired, it can unwind us and fix a poor body. I like to make mine with cider instead of wine, and finish it with apples fried in butter.

SERVES 4

2 tablespoons extra-virgin olive oil

1 large knob of butter

4 firm, large onions, halved and thinly sliced

1 handful of sage leaves, finely chopped

2 bay leaves

2 garlic cloves, peeled and grated

½ glass of cider

good splash of apple brandy

1 litre (35fl oz) beef or chicken stock

salt and freshly ground black pepper

FOR THE GARNISH

4 thick slices of good country bread or sourdough

1 tablespoon extra-virgin olive oil

1 small garlic clove, peeled

1 small knob of butter

2 dessert apples, cut into thick slices

150g (5½oz) mature Cheddar cheese, grated

Set a large heavy-based pan (that has a snug-fitting lid) over a medium–low heat. Add the olive oil and butter and when they're bubbling away throw in the onion slices, breaking up the layers with your fingers as you do so. Add the chopped sage, bay leaves and garlic. Season with salt and pepper and cook, stirring regularly, until the onion begins to caramelize around the edges and is golden and soft and lovely. Then, turn the heat right down and place a lid on the pan. Cook for 25–35 minutes, stirring once or twice during that time.

Remove the lid from the pan and add the cider and the brandy. Bring up to the boil, then add the stock. Bring the soup back to a gentle simmer, stirring regularly. Cook gently, with the lid slightly ajar, for a further 30–40 minutes over a low heat, then season the soup with salt and pepper and keep warm.

Meanwhile, heat the grill to high. To make the garnish, trickle the bread with olive oil and rub with a little garlic. Toast the bread on each side, until golden.

At the same time, set a medium frying pan over a medium heat. Add the butter followed by the apple slices. Fry the apple gently for 3–4 minutes on each side, until the slices are golden around the edges and soft in the middle.

Sprinkle the cheese evenly over the slices of toast and place back under the grill to cook until the cheese is bubbling.

To serve, ladle the hot soup into four warm bowls. Drop a cheese toast into each one and top with a spoonful of buttery apple wedges. Season and serve at once.

roast pheasant with parsnips & chorizo

Although I don't shoot, a lot of people do. In fact, more pheasant may be shot each year than we actually eat. This is a crying shame and should never be allowed to happen. So, friends, if you eat meat, then you should be eating more of this delicious game bird. Pheasants spend the early part of their lives in large, open pens, but once they're strong enough, they are released into the wild, where they live out the rest of their lives. Most of the meat we eat in the UK never gets it this good. I'm a sucker for chorizo. It's such a gregarious, rich sausage. Pair it up with sweet parsnips and the lean pheasant and it becomes something even more fabulous.

SERVES 2

1 oven-ready pheasant (about 800g–1kg/1lb 12oz–2lb 4oz), at room temperature

20g (¾oz) butter, softened

2 large, firm parsnips

4 garlic cloves, skin on and bashed

2 tablespoons extra-virgin olive oil

100g (3½oz) good-quality chorizo sausage, sliced into thick rounds

4 large rosemary sprigs

1 small bunch of thyme sprigs

2–3 bay leaves

salt and freshly ground black pepper

Heat the oven to 200°C/400°F/gas mark 7.

If your pheasant is trussed, cut the string and open up the legs. This will help it cook evenly. Set the bird in the middle of a medium roasting tray, then rub it all over with the butter. Peel the parsnips, then cut each one from top to bottom into four to six lengths, depending on size. If they have fibrous cores, you can cut these out.

Arrange the parsnips around the pheasant, along with the garlic. Trickle the pheasant and parsnips all over with the olive oil and season both the bird and the roots really well.

Place the roasting tray in the oven and cook for 20 minutes, then remove and, using some tongs, carefully turn the parsnips and baste the bird. Tuck in the pieces of chorizo sausage, then tear over all the herbs (placing some in the bird's cavity). Return the tray to the oven and cook for a further 15–20 minutes, until the pheasant is cooked through and the parsnips are lovely and golden and charred in places. To check whether the pheasant is cooked, pierce the leg at the point where it joins the body – if the juices run clear, it's ready. If not, pop back in the oven and test again after a few more minutes.

Once the pheasant is cooked, remove the roasting tray from the oven and allow the bird to rest in a warm place for at least 15 minutes. Serve the pheasant, chorizo and parsnips with boiled cabbage or sprouts.

7.00 P.M. | OCTOBER

Pamela Dixon
now they're all grown up
Marine Parade

a stew of pork, bacon & mushrooms with cream, cider & parsley

I first served this stew aboard a fishing boat out on a big sea on a bloody cold day. I'd cooked it the day before (always a good idea with a stew) and reheated it over a tiny camp stove in the wheel-house. I remember the delicious smells carrying out to the hungry fishermen on deck. Despite the swell, and the rock and roll, I managed to bring out piping hot bowlfuls, and for a moment all you could hear was the wind and the sea. We ended up catching quite a few fish that day, including the unusual looking garfish, which interestingly, has otherworldly green bones.

SERVES 4

dash of extra-virgin olive oil

1 piece of cured pork belly (streaky bacon; about 350g/12oz), cut into 4–5cm (1½–2in) cubes

500g (1lb 2oz) fresh pork belly, cut into 4–5cm (1½–2in) cubes

1 large or 2 small leeks, halved and sliced

2 or 3 garlic cloves, peeled and thinly sliced

4–6 bay leaves

2–3 rosemary sprigs

2–3 thyme sprigs

2 tablespoons plain flour

450ml (16fl oz) cider

450ml (16fl oz) pork, chicken or vegetable stock

knob of butter

250g (9oz) wild or cultivated mushrooms, cut into large pieces

200ml (7fl oz) double cream

small bunch of parsley

salt and freshly ground black pepper

Heat the oven to 150°C/300°F/gas mark 3.

Start by heating the oil in a large heavy-based casserole set over a medium–high heat. Add the cured and fresh pork belly pieces and cook the meat for 6–8 minutes, or until well browned on all sides. Lift the pieces out of the pan using a spatula or slotted spoon and set aside. Add the leeks to the same pan, along with the sliced garlic, all the herbs and a little seasoning. Sweat the leeks gently for about 10 minutes, then return the browned pork pieces to the pan, sprinkle over the plain flour and stir well. Cook for a further 3–4 minutes, then pour in the cider and stock and bring to a simmer. Stir well, then place a tight-fitting lid on the pan and place in the oven for 2 hours, until the pork is fork tender.

Meanwhile, set a large frying pan over a high heat and add the butter. When it's bubbling, add the mushrooms, season them lightly and sauté, turning them regularly, for 6–8 minutes, until cooked through. Set aside.

When the casserole is ready, remove it from the oven and add the fried mushrooms and double cream. Stir well, then return the pan to the oven for 15 minutes without its lid.

Stir in the chopped parsley and check the seasoning before bringing to the table with a sharply dressed green salad and some good bread.

smashed swede with fried sausage, green peppercorns & parmesan

Every time I make this, Alice says: 'Oh my god, I think that's the most delicious thing I've ever eaten.' This is exceptionally good press, particularly for swede, as usually it's a hard-knock life for this middle-of-the-road root. Bringing out the best in anything takes love and encouragement. In this recipe that comes by way of double cream and aged Parmesan. I like to use a nice, fatty, garlicky sausage, but any well-flavoured, free-range sausage will do. Green peppercorns in brine are essential – and they need to be in brine, not dried. They are full of punch and pep and go absolutely perfectly with swede.

SERVES 2

1 swede, cut into large cubes

dash of extra-virgin olive oil

1 large Cumberland sausage

50g (2oz) butter

100ml (3½fl oz) double cream

50g (2oz) Parmesan or hard sheep's cheese, grated

2–3 teaspoons green peppercorns in brine

salt and freshly ground black pepper

Place a large pan of salted water over a high heat and bring to the boil. Add the swede and cook for 30–40 minutes, until the swede is tender.

Meanwhile, set a medium frying pan over a medium heat. Add the dash of oil, followed by the sausage and let it gently sizzle away, turning occasionally, until well browned and cooked through – this should take a good 20 minutes or more. (Cooking the sausage slowly actually helps to tenderise the pork inside and stops it splitting.) Don't be tempted to prick the sausage with a fork – this just lets out all the fat and juices, which are far better kept inside. Keep the sausage warm once cooked.

Once the swede is tender, remove the pan from the heat, drain the swede and leave in the colander to allow the steam to evaporate. Meanwhile, return the pan to a low heat and add the butter and cream. When it's bubbling away, tip in the cooked swede. Use a potato masher to smash and bash the swede into the butter and cream (you could use a potato ricer, if you prefer). The result should be relatively smooth. Stir in all but a smattering of the grated cheese and season well with salt and pepper.

To serve, spoon the swede out over a plate or platter. Top with the sausage, then sprinkle over the green peppercorns. Finish with a sprinkling of the remaining cheese and bring to the table.

spaghetti with bacon, garlic, black pepper & sheep's cheese

When my mum used to work in the evenings or was away for the night, my dad would make this, his favourite spaghetti dish, and one we all loved. Mum was not a fan; for some reason she hated garlic cooked in this way. It was one of very few culinary idiosyncrasies she had. Notes in a curry, whispers at the back of a bolognese or a suggestion in a soup would all be fine, and she cooked with garlic all the time, but it just didn't work for her on this level, unabashed and at the forefront of a dish. We used to open the door to air the kitchen if she was due back. Garlic aside, I'd personally call this a spaghetti masterpiece and one of the easiest pasta recipes I know. Just go big on everything and I think you'll agree.

SERVES 4

200g (7oz) spaghetti

2 tablespoons extra-virgin olive oil

200g (7oz) streaky bacon rashers, cut into small pieces

4 large garlic cloves, peeled and finely grated or chopped

125g (4½oz) hard sheep's cheese (such as pecorino), or Parmesan, finely grated, plus extra for serving

knob of butter

salt and freshly ground black pepper

Bring a large pan of salted water to the boil. Add the spaghetti, stirring once or twice, so it doesn't begin to stick. Cook for 10–12 minutes, or until done to your liking.

Meanwhile, place a large heavy-based frying pan over a medium heat. Add the olive oil, followed by the bacon. Sizzle the bacon for 4–5 minutes, or until all the little bits are beginning to crisp around the edges. Then, add the garlic and cook for a further 1 minute, until the garlic is softened, but not coloured. Remove the pan from the heat while you drain the pasta.

Once you've done this, set the frying pan back on the heat and throw in the cooked spaghetti. Toss the pasta through the bacon, and all that lovely, garlicky fat. Now add the Parmesan and the butter, using a fork to tumble the cheese through it.

Fry the spaghetti and cheese for a few minutes, scraping and scratching at the sticky bits of cheese on the base of the pan with a wooden spatula or spoon. Add plenty of freshly ground back pepper at this point – I always say: when you think you've added enough, add some more. Then, give everything one last turn and serve at once onto warm plates.

a game terrine

I always make this terrine several days before I intend to serve it, because it develops in flavour and always tastes better that way. I layer lean strips of game, as well as a few plump brandy-soaked prunes, within a forcemeat, which I flavour with orange zest, juniper berries and fresh bay. All these flavours go incredibly well with the game, and complement the prunes no end. Serve the terrine in thick slices with toast and chutney.

MAKES 1 LARGE TERRINE

100g (3½oz) stoned prunes

3 tablespoons port

350g (12oz) unsmoked rindless bacon rashers

150g (5½oz) venison liver, trimmed and cubed (use pork liver, if you can't find venison)

250g (9oz) very fatty pork belly, cubed

½ onion, finely diced

2 garlic cloves, peeled and grated

zest of ½ orange

4 thyme sprigs, leaves picked and chopped

3 bay leaves, very finely chopped

1 egg

50g (2oz) white breadcrumbs

200g (7oz) pheasant breast, venison loin or pigeon breast (or a mixture), cut into 3–4cm (1¼–1½in) strips, as long as possible

4 juniper berries, finely chopped

salt and freshly ground black pepper

Place the prunes in a bowl and pour over the port. Leave them to plump up for several hours or overnight. Drain, reserving the port.

To make the forcemeat, roughly chop half the bacon and place it in a large bowl with the venison or pork liver and fatty pork belly. Add the onion, garlic, orange zest, thyme, bay and chopped juniper and mix well. Pass this mixture through a mincer and return it to the bowl. Add the egg, breadcrumbs and reserved port, season and mix everything together.

Stretch out the remaining bacon using the back of a knife to make it as broad and thin as you can. Line a 1 litre (35fl oz) loaf tin or cast-iron terrine with ovensafe cling film, then use the bacon to line the terrine, allowing some overhang on each side. Fill the terrine with a third of the forcemeat. Lay half the game strips along its length and arrange half the prunes around them, as evenly as you can. Add another third of the forcemeat, pressing it down to cover the game and prunes, then arrange another layer of game and prunes. Cover with the remaining forcemeat, pressing it down and levelling it off. Fold over the overhanging bacon and bring the cling film up over the top. Place a lid on the terrine or wrap it in foil nice and tightly.

Heat the oven to 150°C/300°F/gas mark 3. Put the terrine in a large, deep roasting tin, then fill the tin with enough water to come two-thirds up the sides of the terrine and place it in the oven. Cook for 1 hour and 20 minutes, until cooked through.

Remove the terrine from the oven, allow it to cool, then place it in the fridge. Use a weight (a house brick wrapped in cling film works well) to press the terrine overnight – this will give it a better texture. Take the terrine out of the fridge at least 30 minutes before serving in slices with toast and chutney.

squash stuffed with lentils, pheasant & black pudding

This recipe takes these little autumn squashes places they may have only dreamed of when they were sitting quietly growing in the vegetable patch. The red lentil stuffing is so good it's almost a dish in its own right. I start by sweating sweet onions, fragrant rosemary and lots of garlic in butter and olive oil, before adding the lentils, along with a good stock, it's all about building up layers of flavour. I've used pheasant and black pudding because I love them both, but there's no reason why you couldn't use some leftover chicken and good sausage instead, or even rabbit and smoked bacon. If you wanted to make it vegetarian, then finish the lentils with lots of fresh herbs, wilted kale, leeks, and goat's cheese. You can use a variety of different squashes here – I've suggested a few that work well below.

SERVES 4

2 small squashes, such as delicata, acorn, gem or butternut

1 tablespoon extra-virgin olive oil

knob of butter

1 onion, sliced

4 garlic cloves, peeled and grated

2 rosemary sprigs

75g (2½oz) red lentils

400ml (14fl oz) pheasant, chicken or vegetable stock

200g (7oz) leftover roast pheasant or chicken, torn into small shards and pieces

100g (3½oz) good-quality black pudding, cut into bite-size pieces

chives or fennel tops, to finish (optional)

salt and freshly ground black pepper

Heat the oven to 180°C/350°F/gas mark 6.

Depending on the size and shape of the squashes, you can either halve them or slice off their tops. I've done both here and they turn out really well either way. Scoop out and discard the seeds and soft fibres that surround the seeds.

Place the prepared squashes on a roasting tray, cut-sides up, trickle with the olive oil and then season with salt and pepper. Cover the tray loosely with kitchen foil and place in the oven for 45 minutes or until the squash flesh is tender.

Meanwhile, set a medium heavy-based pan over a medium heat. Add the butter and, when it's bubbling, add the onion, garlic and rosemary. Season the onion and stir them as they begin to soften in the pan. After 4–5 minutes, add the red lentils and the stock. Stir well and bring up to a simmer. Cook for 25–30 minutes, until the lentils are tender, then add the leftover pheasant or chicken and the black pudding. Season the mixture really well with salt and pepper, stir, then spoon it into the squashes, and scatter with the chopped herbs, if using. Return the tray to the oven for 15 minutes to heat everything through before serving.

fire planked fish

Cooking is nothing more than a series of questions: 'If I do it this way, what will the outcome be?' At some stage you'll get the answer. But, we're afraid of the unknown; it's just the way we are as people. We're afraid of doing something differently from the way everyone else does it. We're afraid of fire and of things getting burnt. I love this recipe because it challenges the norm; it puts us outside the area we feel comfortable in, and makes us think about food and cooking in another way, in the way we used to. It is a case of managing heat, if the fish doesn't seem to be cooking you move it closer; if the fish catches fire, you put it out.

SERVES 4

100g (3½oz) salt

2 tablespoons golden caster sugar

1 tablespoon crushed black peppercorns

2 teaspoons crushed fennel seeds

2 large fish fillets (such as trout, pollack or whiting), each about 500g (1lb 2oz)

1 large bunch of herbs, such as fennel, dill, parsley and bay (optional)

FOR THE COOKING

a wood fire

2 suitably sized planks of hardwood (at least 60–70cm/24–27in x 15–20cm/6–8in)

some string

Before you begin cooking, you need to soak the first 30cm (12in) or so of each hardwood cooking plank in water for at least 2–3 hours. This will help to stop it catching fire.

To cook the fish, make a cure by combining the salt, sugar, black pepper and fennel seeds in a bowl. Lay the fish fillets side-by-side on a tray and scatter the cure evenly over the two fillets. Leave the fish in the cure for 45–60 minutes, then wash off the salt and pat the fish dry.

Once you've got your wood fire going nicely, lay one fillet on each wooden plank, with the thicker ends of the fillets closer to what will be the bottom of each piece of wood, along with equal amounts of the herbs, if using. Secure them in place with string.

Prop the planks, end up, around the base of a wood fire and let the gentle, smoky heat cook the fish, carefully tending and encouraging the heat to move over the fish, as evenly as you can. This sort of cooking will involve some thought and consideration, but it's definitely worth the effort. Note: if the herbs catch fire, don't worry – that's called flavour, just put them out or let them burn out. If the plank catches fire, similarly, put it out. The fish is cooked when the flesh flakes apart. If the tail end of the fish isn't quite ready at the same time as the lower, thicker part, cut the cooked section away and leave the remainder to finish off in the heat of the fire.

Serve your fish straight away with good bread, homemade mayonnaise (page 220), and a salad.

mussel croquettes

It's impossible to refuse a well-made croquette, irrefutably one of the tastiest canapés of all. These are the most delicious croquettes I've ever eaten. Use fresh, plump mussels and save the cooking liquor, which is packed with flavour, to form the basis of the croquettes. Lovage is a soft, green herb that goes particularly well with mussels; its flavour is somewhere between celery and cumin. If you can't find lovage, flat-leaf parsley will work well.

MAKES 8–12

50g (2oz) butter, plus a small knob of butter for frying

½ tablespoon extra-virgin olive oil

1 large shallot or small onion, finely diced

1 garlic clove, peeled and grated

1kg (2lb 4oz) mussels, cleaned and debearded (discard any with broken or open shells)

125g (4½oz) plain flour

50ml (2fl oz) double cream

1 tablespoon chopped lovage or parsley

1 egg, beaten

100g (3½oz) white breadcrumbs

light vegetable oil, such as sunflower, for deep frying

salt and freshly ground black pepper

Set a large pan over a medium heat, add the knob of butter and the olive oil and, when bubbling, add the diced shallot or onion and the garlic. Cook for 3–4 minutes, until the shallot or onion is soft but not coloured. Turn up the heat to high and add the mussels along with a splash of water, a pinch of salt and a twist of black pepper. Place a lid on the pan and cook for 2–4 minutes to allow the shells to open up. Tip the mussels and all the liquid into a large bowl, discard any shells that remain closed, and allow to cool. Once cool, scoop out the mussels from the cooking liquid using a slotted spoon. Reserve 200ml (7fl oz) of the cooking liquid and as many of the lovely diced shallots as you can. Remove the mussel meat from each shell and roughly chop.

Melt the 50g (2oz) of butter in a small saucepan over a medium heat, add 50g (2oz) of the flour and cook it out for 1–2 minutes. Gradually, add the reserved mussel-cooking liquor, stirring all the time. Bring to a simmer and stir until it is very thick and bubbling. Add the cream, the chopped mussels, and the herbs and season with salt and pepper. Stir well and remove from the heat. Spoon out the mixture over a plate lined with a large sheet of cling film. Fold the excess cling film over the top of the mixture and place in the fridge to chill until set firm.

Once the mixture has set, shape it into balls or quenelles. Dip each one into the remaining flour, followed by the beaten egg, then roll in breadcrumbs until well coated. Pour enough oil into a deep saucepan to come 10cm (4in) up the sides. Heat the vegetable oil to 180°C/350°F, or until a cube of white bread turns golden within a minute. Deep-fry the croquettes until browned and crisp (about 3–4 minutes), then remove with a slotted spoon and drain on kitchen paper. Serve hot, but not boiling hot.

baked apples with vanilla, butter, lemon & brown sugar

Baking apples takes cooking away from what it means today. It takes it away from this culture of confusion and noise; it takes it away from the restaurants and the screens; it takes it away from the business it's become. Baking apples takes cooking home again, to a place where only the act matters and where we want nothing but love, and for the skin to split and open and the fruit to become soft.

SERVES 2–3

3 or 4 dessert apples, such as Cox's or russet

50g (2oz) unsalted butter, softened

1 vanilla pod, split and seeds scraped

2 tablespoons soft brown sugar

pared zest of 1 lemon

double cream, to serve (optional)

Heat the oven to 180°C/350°F/gas mark 6.

Halve the apples (I like to leave in the core) and arrange them in the middle of a sheet of baking parchment large enough to be able to fold over the apples to encase them in a parcel.

Place the butter in a small bowl, add the vanilla seeds and sugar, and mix well. Dot a little of this sweet vanilla butter over the top of each apple. Scatter over the lemon zest and chuck the vanilla pod on for good measure. Fold the parchment carefully over the apples to create a nice, neat parcel, then tie the parcel with some string to hold the paper in place.

Place the apples on a baking tray and place in the oven. Bake for about 20–25 minutes, until cooked through.

Remove the tray from the oven and carefully open the steamy parchment parcel. Serve the hot apples and all their lemony, vanilla-y, buttery juices with a generous lick of double cream, if you wish.

plum & almond tart with star anise & vanilla

There's something really nice about the word 'plum'. It feels good in the mouth when you say it. Your tongue and lips have to move in a certain way to make the sound... plum. In fact, the feel of it is so nice that, at one point, the word for the sweet, juicy fruit was used to describe literally anything desirable. Here, I'm baking plums in a rather sticky, greedy, almond tart, flavoured with star anise, a spice that has cool, sweet, aromatic undertones and complements the plum beautifully.

SERVES 8–10

4 tablespoons plum jam

6–8 ripe plums, halved and destoned

handful of flaked almonds

FOR THE PASTRY

90g (3¼oz) icing sugar

340g (11¾oz) plain flour, plus extra for dusting

170g (6oz) butter, cubed and chilled, plus extra for greasing

1 egg

2 tablespoons iced water

FOR THE FRANGIPANE

110g (3¾oz) unsalted butter

110g (3¾oz) golden caster sugar

½ vanilla pod, split and seeds scraped

2 star anise, finely crushed

3 eggs, beaten

110g (3¾oz) ground almonds

First, make the pastry. Combine the icing sugar and plain flour in a medium bowl. Rub in the chilled butter cubes until the mixture resembles fine breadcrumbs (you can also do this in a food processor). Add in the egg and iced water, and stir through to combine. Tip out the dough onto a lightly floured surface and bring it together with your hands, kneading lightly to achieve a smooth finish. Wrap the pastry tightly in cling film and place it in the fridge to rest for at least 30 minutes.

Heat the oven to 180°C/350°F/gas mark 6. On a lightly floured surface, roll out the pastry until it is about 2–3mm (1⁄16–⅛in) thick. Grease and flour a 28cm (11¼in) round, loose-bottomed tart tin, then lay over the pastry, tucking it into the corners of the tin and leaving an overhang. Line the pastry case with baking parchment and baking beans and blind bake the tart case for 25 minutes, then remove the baking beans and parchment, trim the overhang, and return to the oven for 10 minutes, or until the base is just starting to colour. Remove and set aside, but leave the oven on.

For the frangipane, cream the butter, caster sugar, vanilla seeds and star anise until light and fluffy. Add the eggs and ground almonds, and mix until combined. Set aside.

To make the tart, spread the plum jam over the base of the pastry case, then spoon over the frangipane mix. Arrange the plums over the frangipane, cut-side down, pushing them in lightly with your fingers. Finally, scatter over the flaked almonds. Bake the tart in the oven for 25–35 minutes, or until golden and set on the outside and still a little soft in the middle. Cool for 30 minutes before serving.

VEGETARIAN

an apple tart

I like to make my own rough puff pastry for this traditional French apple tart. The results are very similar to a classic puff, but it's much quicker to make. The pastry is covered with a layer of fragrant, brambly apple compôte, which I like to perfume with lemon zest and bay as it bubbles away gently in the pan. It should have an almost fluffy texture when cooked. Finally, the compôte gets topped by thinly sliced dessert apples, which hold their shape as the tart bakes. It's the combination of the crisp, flaky pastry alongside the sweet, moist compôte that makes this simple tart so heavenly. Serve it warm with double cream, custard or a good vanilla ice cream; or cold with a cup of hot tea or coffee.

SERVES 8

1 large bramley apple (about 400g/14oz), peeled, cored and finely sliced

juice of 1 lemon and zest of ½

2 bay leaves

100g (3½oz) golden caster sugar

4–6 dessert apples, depending on size

FOR THE ROUGH PUFF PASTRY

150g (5½oz) unsalted butter, chilled and cut into small cubes

300g (10½oz) plain flour, plus extra for dusting

good pinch of salt

about 100ml (3½fl oz) iced water

First, make the pastry. In a bowl, combine the butter cubes with the flour and salt, then add just enough iced water to bring everything together into a dough full of big pieces of butter. On a well-floured surface, roll out the dough in one direction, away from you, to a rectangle about 1cm (½in) thick. Fold the two short ends into the middle so they overlap. Give the pastry a quarter-turn, and repeat the rolling and folding process three more times. Wrap the pastry in cling film, then rest it in the fridge for 30 minutes. Remove the pastry from the fridge and repeat the folding process a further three times. Wrap the pastry again and place it in the fridge to chill.

Put the apple slices in a pan with the lemon zest, bay leaves and 75g (2½oz) of the sugar. Add 1 tablespoon of water, then cook, covered, over a low heat, stirring regularly, until the apple pieces have dissolved and you have a thick, slightly translucent purée – about 30 minutes. Spoon into a bowl, cool, then place in the fridge to chill.

Heat the oven to 190°C/375°F/gas mark 6½. Roll out the pastry on a well-floured sheet of baking parchment to about 4–5mm (⅛–¼in) thick. Take a large, circular plate (about 30cm/12in diameter) and use it as a guide to cut out a pastry round. Remove the trim and use the parchment to slide the round onto a large baking tray. Spread the chilled apple purée evenly over the top of the pastry, almost to the edges. Discard the bay leaves. Arrange the apple slices over the purée in overlapping concentric circles, working from the outside in, until you have used them all up. Bake the tart for 30–40 minutes, or until the pastry is risen and crisp and the apples are soft and golden. Cool the tart for 15–20 minutes before serving.

VEGETARIAN

lentil dhal with crispy kale

A well-made dhal is a complete treasure; it is a bowl of soft gold. A dhal can warm us like a fire, with its spice; and it can soothe and comfort us, like a favourite blanket might have done in the past. This dhal is nothing more than a few handfuls of red lentils that have been gently simmered with some lovely spices. However, it always amazes me how much depth and flavour it has. I like to serve piping-hot bowlfuls with crispy kale (its light, brittle texture works so well here), warm boiled eggs, and some fermented cabbage (page 170). Together they make a quite wonderful winter supper.

SERVES 4–6

1 bunch of curly kale, stalks removed

1 tablespoon extra-virgin olive oil

1 tablespoon coconut oil

1 onion, sliced

3 large garlic cloves, peeled and thinly sliced

½ thumb-sized piece of ginger, peeled and grated

1 hot red chilli, deseeded and thinly sliced

½ tablespoon cumin seeds, coarsely crushed

½ tablespoon coriander seeds, coarsely crushed

2 cardamom pods, bashed

2 teaspoons black mustard seeds

2 teaspoons black onion seeds

1 tablespoon curry powder

250g (9oz) red lentils

1 litre (35fl oz) well-flavoured vegetable stock

soft-boiled eggs, natural yoghurt, toasted seeds (page 96) and fresh chilli, to serve

salt and freshly ground black pepper

Heat the oven to 110°C/225°F/gas mark ½. First, make the crispy kale. Wash the kale leaves, then spin them in a salad spinner until they're really dry. Place the leaves in a bowl with the olive oil and a good pinch of salt. Using your hands, mix the leaves well to coat in the oil. Line a baking tray with baking parchment, then arrange the kale in an even layer on the tray and place it in the oven. Bake for 25–30 minutes, turning the individual leaves once or twice during cooking, until they are nice and crisp. Remove the leaves from the oven and allow to cool.

Heat a large, heavy-based pan over a low–medium heat. Add the coconut oil and, when hot, add the onion, garlic, ginger, chilli, cumin, coriander, cardamom, black mustard and onion seeds, and curry powder. Cook, stirring regularly, for 8–10 minutes, until the onion is soft but not coloured.

Place the lentils in a sieve and give them a quick rinse, then add them to the pan with the onion mixture and fry them for a few moments. Add the stock, bring the liquid to a gentle simmer and cook, stirring regularly, for 35–40 minutes, until the lentils are soft and the dhal has thickened. If things look a little dry at any time, add a splash more stock or water. Season the dhal well with salt and pepper, remove from the heat and bring to the table. To serve, spoon the dhal into warm bowls and top with the kale. I love this with a soft boiled egg, a spoonful of natural yoghurt, and some toasted seeds sprinkled over.

my favourite pizza

There is usually a time and a place for good pizza. More often than not, it's a Friday night for me, at home with a glass of something red and a good film. But, I'd take this one, happily, any day of the week.

MAKES 3 X 30CM (12IN) PIZZAS

FOR THE TOMATO SAUCE

1 tablespoon extra-virgin olive oil

2 garlic cloves, peeled and sliced

1 x 400g (14oz) tin good-quality chopped tomatoes

1 teaspoon sugar

1 bay leaf

salt and freshly ground black pepper

FOR THE BASE

500g (1lb 2oz) strong bread flour, plus extra for dusting

10g (¼oz) salt

2 tablespoons extra-virgin olive oil, plus extra for greasing

1 teaspoon instant dried yeast

320ml (11fl oz) lukewarm water

FOR THE TOPPING (PER PIZZA)

3–4 tablespoons tomato sauce

1 ball of mozzarella, torn

100g (3½oz) chestnut or Portobello mushrooms, sliced thinly

½ small red onion, sliced thinly

75g (2½oz) blue cheese, crumbled

2 or 3 thyme sprigs, leaves picked

extra-virgin olive oil

salt and freshly ground black pepper

First, make the sauce. Heat a medium pan over a medium heat. Add the olive oil and, when hot, add the sliced garlic. Sizzle the garlic for 30 seconds or so, then add the chopped tomatoes, half a tin of water, the sugar and the bay leaf. Cook, stirring regularly, for 30–40 minutes, then season with salt and pepper to taste. Set aside.

While the sauce is cooking, start the base. Place the flour, salt and olive oil in the bowl of a food processor fitted with a dough hook. In a jug, combine the yeast with the water and whisk to dissolve. Pour this over the flour and switch on the machine. Allow it to run for 4–5 minutes, until the dough is soft, smooth and pliable. (Alternatively, roll up your sleeves and knead your dough by hand for 10–12 minutes on a lightly floured work surface.)

Lightly grease a bowl with olive oil and pop in the dough. Cover with a damp tea towel and allow the dough to prove for 3–4 hours at room temperature or overnight in the fridge.

Preheat the oven to 240°C/475°F/gas mark 9½, if it goes that high, or at least 220°C/425°F/gas mark 9. Place a baking sheet or pizza stone (or three if you have room) inside to warm up.

Turn out the dough onto a lightly floured surface, knock it back, then let it rest for a minute or two before dividing into three. Dust the dough with more flour, then roll out each ball nice and thinly. Carefully remove the hot sheet or pizza stone from the oven and lay a piece of rolled dough onto it. Then, top the pizza as quickly as you can. I'd suggest, tomato sauce first, then mozzarella, mushrooms, onion, blue cheese and thyme. Finally, give the whole lot a generous trickle of olive oil and season well. Bake the pizza for 10–12 minutes, or until crisp and golden at the edges – even a little charred in places. Serve straight away, and repeat with the remaining dough.

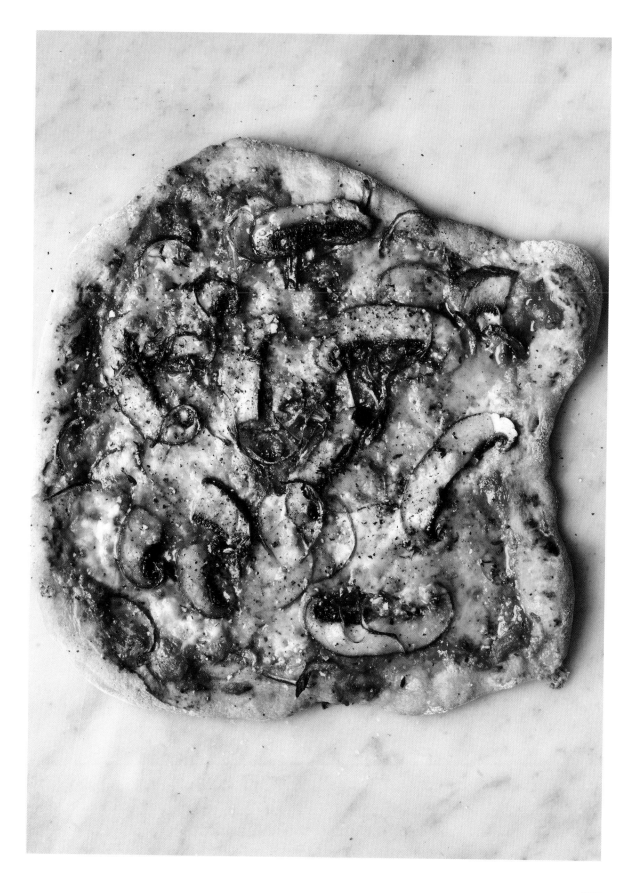

slow-roast goat with honey, saffron, prunes & preserved lemon

Goat and kid have had a renaissance in recent years, and rightly so. The meat is delicious – and it's ethically sound. Many billy goats (a by-product of the dairy industry), which were once killed at birth, are now reared for meat. If you like the depth of flavour in lamb and mutton, then goat will definitely be your jam. Saffron, cumin and cardamom add character to this rich braise, while cinnamon, prunes and honey bring gorgeous sweetness.

SERVES 4–6

½ cinnamon stick

2 teaspoons cumin seeds

2 teaspoons coriander seeds

6 cardamom pods

1 teaspoon ground turmeric

½ goat leg (about 800g–1kg/1lb 12oz–2lb 4oz), boned and rolled

4 tablespoons extra-virgin olive oil

2 onions, finely sliced

4 garlic cloves, peeled and finely sliced

1 red chilli, deseeded and thinly sliced

1 thumb-sized piece of ginger, peeled and grated

2 tablespoons tomato purée

200g (7oz) juicy prunes, stoned

pinch of saffron threads

1 preserved lemon, skin thickly sliced, flesh discarded

4 bay leaves

1 small bunch of thyme, torn

1 small bunch of mint, leaves picked and chopped

pinch of smoked paprika, to serve

1–2 tablespoons runny honey

salt and freshly ground black pepper

Heat the oven to 200°C/400°F/gas mark 7. Place the cinnamon, cumin, coriander, and cardamom pods in a small pan over a medium heat. Toast for 1–2 minutes, until fragrant, then tip them into a mortar and use the pestle to coarsely crush. Pick out and discard the cardamom husks, which are tricky to grind well.

Combine the crushed spices with the turmeric and plenty of salt and pepper. Rub the goat leg with half the olive oil, then work the dry spice mix into the meat, making sure you get it in all the nooks and crannies. Place the goat leg on a suitable roasting tray and place in the hot oven for 25–30 minutes, until browned.

Meanwhile, set a large cast-iron pot (with a lid) over a medium heat. Add the remaining olive oil and, when it's hot, add the onions, garlic, chilli and ginger and cook, stirring regularly, for 10–12 minutes. Add the tomato purée, prunes, saffron, preserved lemon, bay leaves and 1 glass of water and stir well. Bring to a gentle simmer.

When the goat leg is nice and brown, lift it out of the oven and carefully place it in the pot. Scatter around the thyme, place on the lid and put the pot in the oven. Lower the heat to 150°C/300°F/gas mark 3 and cook for 2½ hours, until the meat is tender and giving. (Check the pot from time to time, and if it's looking dry, top it up with a splash more water.) Remove from the oven and allow the goat to rest for 15–20 minutes before serving.

To serve, sprinkle with chopped mint and a pinch of paprika and trickle with honey, then bring the pot to the table and enjoy with with flat breads and a salad.

5.00 P.M. | NOVEMBER

tea with Simon & Ines
New House

roast turbot & chicken wings

Turbot, the most revered of flat fish, brims with character and charm. It is a king, made of pure, white muscle and is meatier than the majority of wretched meat we eat everyday. This beautiful fish should never be anything other than the rarest of treats. Chicken wings, on the other hand, are underappreciated, even considered second rate. But, I think, if they're cooked in the correct way, they are the best part of the bird. Nothing rivals them in flavour or texture: they're ratio perfected – skin to meat, meat to moisture, moisture to crunch. So, for me, it made complete sense to pair up these two wonderful ingredients. It is simply a case of equality.

SERVES 2
(OR 4 AS A STARTER)

8 chicken wings

2 tablespoons extra-virgin olive oil

3–4 rosemary sprigs

3–4 thyme sprigs

4 pieces of turbot fillet (about 400g/14oz), skin on

salt and freshly ground black pepper

Heat the oven to 180°C/350°F/gas mark 6.

Place the chicken wings in a large roasting tin. Trickle over the olive oil and throw in the herbs. Season well with salt and pepper, then tumble everything together. Place in the oven and roast for 1 hour, turning once or twice.

Take the tray out of the oven and use some tongs to remove the wings to a plate. Turn the fish through the hot, salty chicken fat to coat, then arrange in the tray, skin-side down. Return the wings to the tray and place the whole lot back in the oven for 10–12 minutes, until the fish is just cooked through.

Serve at once with a crisp, green salad.

whole beef shin with red wine, carrots & little onions

Our lifestyles can be so frenetic that it can be hard to find a moment to step out of the grind and slow down the rhythms. Taking time to make something good to eat is actually a great way to do this; I'd go so far as to say, it's form of recovery. This recipe is gentle and warming and perfect for those slower, darker nights at home. I like to use whole shin of beef on the bone. Ask your butcher for it, I find it's the best cut for cooking in this way.

SERVES 4

dash of oil or beef dripping, for frying

150g (5½oz) chunky bacon lardons

2 thick slices of shin beef, on the bone (about 800g/1lb 12oz)

2 tablespoons plain flour

1 large knob of butter

8 small carrots, peeled but left whole

12 little onions or small shallots, peeled but left whole

200g (7oz) small chestnut mushrooms, halved

1 onion, halved and finely sliced

2 small celery sticks, finely sliced

2 garlic cloves, peeled and thinly sliced

3 or 4 thyme sprigs

2 bay leaves

400ml (14fl oz) red wine

400ml (14fl oz) beef, chicken or vegetable stock

salt and freshly ground black pepper

Heat the oven to 150°C/300°F/gas mark 3. Heat a large heavy-based frying pan over a medium–high heat and add the oil or dripping. Scatter in the bacon lardons and fry them for 3–5 minutes on all sides, until they are beginning to crisp a little around the edges. Remove to a plate while you turn your attention to the beef. Dust the pieces of shin in the flour, and then place them in the same hot pan. Season the beef all over with salt and pepper and fry for 3–4 minutes on each side, and for a few minutes on the thick edges if you can, to brown all over. Remove the beef and set it aside.

Leave the pan on the heat. Add the butter, then the carrots and baby onions, and fry them gently on all sides for about 8–10 minutes, until they have taken on a little colour. Set these aside on a clean plate. Add the mushrooms to the pan, season them lightly and fry for 6–8 minutes. Set these aside with the carrots and baby onions.

Keep the pan on the heat and add the sliced onion, celery and garlic, and the thyme and bay. Season, then sweat the vegetables gently for about 4–6 minutes, until they begin to soften.

Return the bacon lardons and shin to the pan and turn up the heat. Pour in the wine and bring to the boil. Add the stock (it should just cover the meat) and bring back to a gentle simmer, stirring once or twice. Put a lid on the pan and cook the shin for about 3–4 hours, or until the meat is tender. Then, add the carrots, mushrooms and onions and stir. Replace the lid and return to the oven for a further 35–40 minutes, until both the carrots and onions are tender. Remove the stew from the oven, adjust the seasoning, then let stand for 20 minutes before eating. (It will be even better after 24 hours.)

roast bream with artichokes, onions, smoked bacon & thyme

It is winter. As I write this I'm sitting at my desk looking out over the bay. The crumpled grey sea liquefies a grey sky; my body remembers August. Every day the little trawler makes its way home. I see her now beyond the black pine. On the shortest days of the year, I'll only see the pitch of her riding light. Last night I cooked this dish using black bream. It was probably one of the most delicious 'all-in-one' recipes I've made for years. I stop and wonder whether the little trawler caught any bream today.

SERVES 4

500g (1lb 2oz) Jerusalem artichokes, peeled and cut into large pieces

2 red onions, cut into wedges

250g (9oz) smoked bacon lardons

1 small bunch of fresh thyme

4 garlic cloves, bashed but not peeled

2 tablespoons extra-virgin olive oil

1 large bream or other white fish (about 1kg/2lb 4oz), scaled and gutted

salt and freshly ground black pepper

Preheat the oven to 180°C/350°F/gas mark 6.

Take a large, heavy roasting dish or tray and scatter over the artichokes, onion wedges, bacon lardons, thyme, and garlic cloves. Trickle over the olive oil and season well with salt and pepper. Use a piece of baking parchment to cover the dish loosely to stop anything colouring too quickly, then roast for 35–45 minutes, or until the artichokes are tender, turning everything once or twice during the cooking time. (Note that the cooking time can vary quite dramatically with these little tubers.)

Once the artichokes are tender, remove them from the oven. Slash the fish three or four times on each side, and lay it on top of the artichokes. Use a spoon to baste the fish in some of the bacon fat from the bottom of the dish, then season the fish with salt and pepper. Turn the fish over and repeat the process.

Return the dish to the oven and bake for a further 20 minutes, or until the fish is just cooked through. You can check this by inserting the tip of a sharp knife into one of the slashes and teasing the flesh from the bone. If it comes away with ease, it's cooked. Bring the whole tray to the table and let everyone help themselves.

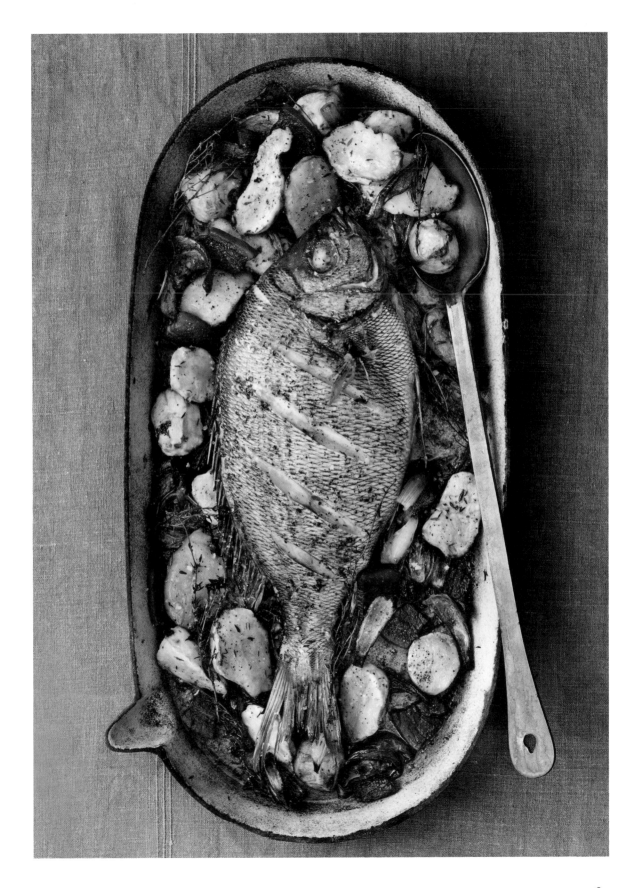

286

roast purple sprouting broccoli with anchovy, cream, chilli & parmesan

Purple sprouting broccoli is at its best in deepest winter. When it's dark and the weather is bitter and wicked, this plant will flourish and, as if in defiance, become sweeter with it. There are a lot of delicious ways to cook this superb brassica, but recently I've been roasting it, which accentuates its already deep quality. This dish combines a handful of big flavours that all complement the broccoli beautifully. Everyone who's tasted this dish has gone back for more.

SERVES 2 AS A MAIN
OR 4 AS A SIDE

400g (14oz) chunky purple sprouting broccoli

3 tablespoons extra-virgin olive oil

1 knob of butter

2 or 3 garlic cloves, peeled and thinly sliced

8 anchovy fillets

1 small red chilli, thinly sliced

4 rosemary sprigs, leaves picked and chopped

200ml (7fl oz) double cream

25g (1oz) Parmesan or hard sheep's cheese, finely grated

salt and freshly ground black pepper

Heat the oven to 200°C/400°F/gas mark 7.

Trim and discard any coarser fibrous ends from the broccoli spears, then lay the tender parts out across a baking tray. Season with salt and pepper and trickle with 2 tablespoons of the olive oil. Place the broccoli in the hot oven and roast for 20–25 minutes, turning once or twice during cooking, until the thickest part of the stem is tender.

While the broccoli is roasting, set a small pan over a medium heat. Add the remaining oil and the butter and when it's bubbling away, add the garlic, anchovies, chilli and rosemary. Sizzle the ingredients for 3–4 minutes, until the anchovies start to melt into the butter and the garlic starts to just toast around the edges. Pour in the cream and bring up to a simmer. Turn down the heat and allow the cream to reduce by a third, or until it's nice and thick (about 3–4 minutes).

As soon as the broccoli has cooked, remove it from the oven, spoon over the anchovy dressing and finish with a scattering of grated Parmesan cheese. Serve immediately.

grilled oysters with salsify & ham

There's so much more to the beautiful oyster than a brief sensual swallow. A cooked oyster, whether it's crisply fried, gently poached or cooked slowly in a pie, can be just as exciting. One of my favourite ways to eat oysters is grilled, fiercely, in a small sea of bubbling butter, crushed garlic, parsley and breadcrumb. If you're not a fan of oysters in the raw, please try them this way. Here, I'm taking that idea and building on it, adding two other ingredients I really love. Salsify, known as 'the oyster plant' (it tastes nothing like oysters, but seems fitting), is a slender, delicately flavoured root, with a gorgeous creamy texture and a distinct nuttiness, and pairs with the oysters incredibly well. The other ingredient is ham: slices of tender salty air-dried ham tie the dish together in the same way copper rivets tie the hull of a ship or the ocean ties one piece of land to the next.

SERVES 2

8–10 live oysters

6 salsify, peeled

2 tablespoons extra-virgin olive oil

40g (1½oz) butter

1 rosemary sprig

pinch of chilli flakes

1 large garlic clove, peeled and grated

1 small bunch of parsley

25g (1oz) white breadcrumbs

about 100g (3½oz) thinly sliced air-dried ham

salt and freshly ground black pepper

To shuck an oyster you'll need an oyster knife (one with a sturdy, short blade) and a tea towel to protect your hand from the sharp shell. Hold the oyster firmly, cupped-side down in the tea towel on a chopping board, with the shell's hinge facing towards you. Insert the knife tip downwards between the two halves of the shell at the pointed back end, at the hinge. Lever the shell open a little, then slip the knife along the underside of the top half of the shell, severing the oyster's adductor muscle and fully opening the shell. Carefully slide the knife blade underneath the oyster to release it completely. Try to save any liquor in the shell. Shuck the oysters one by one, leaving them in the shell in their juices while you prepare the rest of the dish.

Bring a pan of salted water to the boil. Cook the salsify for 8–10 minutes, until tender, then drain. Cut the salsify into 10cm (4in) pieces and place in a shallow roasting tray. Trickle over the olive oil and dot over half the butter. Pour over the oyster juices, tear over the rosemary and season with the chilli flakes and some black pepper.

Warm the remaining butter in a small pan over a medium heat. When bubbling, add the garlic and cook for 30 seconds, then add the parsley and breadcrumbs. Turn to coat, then remove from the heat.

Heat the grill to medium. Sit the oysters among the salsify, then top each one with some buttery breadcrumbs. Place the tray under the grill for 4–5 minutes, or until the breadcrumbs are crisp and golden. Tear the ham over the oysters and salsify and bring to the table.

taramasalata, crackling & kale

I stand by the kitchen table. You look at me and say: I've been hungry all my life. I try to name it, make it a thing, but my words thicken. You say: a memory doesn't need a name. As you lean in, I see bits of wildness in you.

SERVES 6–8

300–400g (10½–14oz) pork skin from the shoulder or loins, with 5mm (¼in) of fat on its underside

1 bunch of red Russian or Tuscan curly kale, tough stalks removed

1 tablespoon extra-virgin olive oil

salt and freshly ground black pepper

FOR THE TARAMASALATA

3–4 thick slices of stale country bread or sourdough

about 200ml (7fl oz) whole milk

250g (9oz) smoked cod roe

1 small garlic clove, peeled and grated

150ml (5fl oz) good-quality extra-virgin olive oil

150ml (5fl oz) sunflower oil

juice of ½ lemon

Begin by making the taramasalata. Tear up the bread and place it in a bowl, pour over the milk and allow the bread to soak for about 5 minutes. Place the roe on a board and use a sharp knife to split the skin across the roe. Take a spoon and carefully scoop out the tender roe into a food processor. Squeeze out the excess milk from the bread and add the soaked bread to the roe, along with the grated garlic. Combine the oils in a jug, then switch on the machine and gradually trickle them in, a little at a time. The principle here is similar to making mayonnaise: once all the oil has been combined, add the lemon juice and taste – it shouldn't need seasoning. (If it becomes too thick – which can happen – add a little water to loosen.)

To get the best crackling, it's really important that the pork skin is dry to the touch. Keep it uncovered on the bottom shelf of the fridge overnight, or even for a couple of days. When you're ready to cook the crackling, heat the oven to 230–240°C/450–475°F/gas mark 9.

Place the dry skin, fat-side down on a board. Take a sharp knife and cut the skin into 3–4cm (1¼–1½in) strips. Place a metal rack over a roasting tray and lay the strips of skin on top, fat-side down. Season all over with salt, then place in the oven for 15–25 minutes, or until the crackling is puffed and popped, light and golden. If it's not quite there after this time, turn down the oven to 180°C/350°F/gas mark 6 and cook for a further 10–15 minutes, or until you think it's done. Remove from the oven and set aside to keep warm.

Reduce the oven temperature to 100°C/200°F/gas mark ½. Toss the kale leaves in 1 tablespoon of olive oil and a good pinch of salt. Arrange the leaves in a single layer over one or more large baking trays. Bake for 30–35 minutes, turning once or twice, until the kale is glass brittle. Spoon the taramasalata into a bowl, season with pepper, if you like, and serve with the crackling and kale for dipping.

treacle tart with thyme & orange

My grandfather, Digby, spent part of the war stationed down in Weymouth, an old harbour town in Dorset. He helped to man a fort, which looked out over Portland Harbour, then home to an important Royal Navy base. The fort was heavily armoured and had big guns. Should any threat approach, Digby would be ready. Now... stories can change with time, but I was told that when a fleet of German bombers flew over the fort, Digby and his men were in a local tea room, eating treacle tart.

SERVES 8–10

725g (1lb 9½oz) golden syrup

1 egg

50ml (2fl oz) double cream

50g (2oz) unsalted butter

zest of 1 orange

2 teaspoons thyme leaves, chopped, plus an extra thyme sprig, to decorate

200g (7oz) white breadcrumbs

FOR THE PASTRY

45g (1½oz) icing sugar

170g (6oz) plain flour, plus extra for dusting

85g (3oz) butter, cubed and chilled, plus extra for greasing

1 tablespoon iced water

1 egg, plus an extra beaten egg for egg washing

First, make the pastry. Combine the icing sugar and plain flour in a medium bowl. Rub in the chilled butter cubes until the mixture resembles fine breadcrumbs (you can also do this in a food processor). Add in the iced water and the egg, and stir through to combine. Tip out the dough and bring it together with your hands, kneading lightly to achieve a smooth finish. Wrap the pastry tightly in cling film and place it in the fridge to rest for at least 30 minutes.

Heat the oven to 180°C/350°F/gas mark 6. On a lightly floured surface, roll out the pastry until it is about 2mm (1/16in) thick. Grease and flour a 3cm-deep (1¼in) x 22cm (8½in) loose-bottomed tart tin, then lay over the pastry, tucking it into the corners and leaving an overhang. Line the pastry case with baking parchment and baking beans. Blind bake the pastry for 25 minutes, then remove the paper and beans, trim the overhang and brush the pastry with beaten egg. Return to the oven for 10 minutes, until the base is just colouring. Remove and set aside, but leave the oven on.

To make the filling, pour the golden syrup into a medium pan set over a low heat. Whisk the egg and cream together in a bowl. When the syrup is hot, but not boiling, stir in the butter and allow it to melt. Then, stir in the orange zest, chopped thyme, breadcrumbs, and the cream and egg mixture. Take the pan off the heat and let it stand for 5 minutes, to allow the breadcrumbs to take up the syrup.

Pour the filling into the pastry case and bake for 35–40 minutes, until just set and golden brown around the edges. Leave to cool in the tin for 15–20 minutes before transferring to a serving plate, decorating with a thyme sprig and bringing to the table.

VEGETARIAN

fudge, raisin & hazelnut brittle parfait

This pudding is for those with a sweet tooth. It's basically frozen meringue, embellished with double cream and laced with raisins, fudge and praline. As a result it's incredibly naughty and not for the faint of heart. I'd enjoy eating this on the sofa with a blanket and a decent film, as much as I would with a black coffee, after a good supper with friends.

SERVES 12

50g (2oz) hazelnuts

300g (10½oz) caster sugar

good pinch of flaky salt

6 egg whites, at room temperature

300ml (10½fl oz) double cream

1 vanilla pod, split and seeds scraped

150g (5½oz) soft fudge, cut into small pieces

1 good handful of plump raisins

Heat the oven to 175°C/330°F/gas mark 6.

To make the hazelnut brittle, place the hazelnuts in an ovenproof dish and roast for about 10 minutes, then place them in a clean tea towel and vigorously rub them to remove the skins.

Place 75g (2½oz) of the sugar in a smallish heavy-based pan and set it over a medium heat. Leave it until the edges start to liquefy, resisting the urge to stir it. It will melt unevenly at first, but a little shake and a swirl of the pan at this point will help. When the sugar is an even, light golden colour add the skinned hazelnuts and the salt and stir them in to coat. Pour the contents of the pan out over a non-stick baking sheet or oiled tray and allow to cool. Crush up the cooled nuts into small pieces. I use the end of a rolling pin for this job.

Whisk the egg whites, until they begin to form soft peaks. Add the remaining sugar, a little at a time, and continue whisking until you have a soft, smooth meringue. In a separate bowl whisk the cream with the vanilla seeds until just beginning to thicken. The whisk should leave ribbons that disappear after a few moments. Fold the cream into the meringue, followed by the pieces of hazelnut brittle, the fudge pieces and the raisins.

Line a 1 litre (35fl oz) loaf tin or terrine with cling film, leaving plenty of overhang. Spoon in the mixture, level it out, then fold over the overhanging cling film. Place in the freezer for 24 hours.

To serve, cut or spoon the pudding out onto individual plates or into bowls and serve immediately.

9.30 P.M. | FEBRUARY

Mew's house
Wootton Fitzpaine

chocolate, fudge & smoked salt cookies

I like to serve these cookies warm from the oven after supper, with a coffee or a brandy, or both. You can make the dough in advance; simply roll it into a cylinder, wrap it in baking parchment and pop it in the fridge. You can then slice off individual rounds for baking whenever you feel like it. The pinch of smoked salt adds wisps of warmth to the bitter chocolate and sweet fudge, and gives the cookies an almost campfire quality.

MAKES 8–10 LARGE COOKIES

100g (3½oz) unsalted butter

100g (3½oz) light soft brown sugar

50g (2oz) caster sugar

1 egg

dash of vanilla extract or the seeds from ½ a vanilla pod

150g (5½oz) self-raising flour

75g (2½oz) good-quality dark chocolate (70% cocoa solids), broken up

75g (2½oz) your favourite fudge

1 or 2 good pinches of smoked salt flakes

Heat the oven to 190°C/375°F/gas mark 6½ and line two baking sheets with baking parchment.

Melt the butter in a small saucepan over a low heat. Put both types of sugar into a mixing bowl, pour on the butter and beat well. Add the egg and the vanilla extract or seeds and beat again until well combined. Sift in the flour and fold it in. Allow the mixture to cool for 15–20 minutes before stirring in half the chocolate and half the fudge pieces.

Dot heaped spoonfuls of the mixture over the prepared trays, then distribute the remaining chocolate and fudge equally over the surfaces of the cookies. Sprinkle the cookies with the smoked salt and bake for 8–10 minutes, until the cookies are lovely and golden. Allow the cookies to cool for 10 minutes before lifting onto a cooling rack to firm up. Store in an airtight container for up to 1 week.

rhubarb cooked with rose geranium leaves

Alice grows rose pelargonium (*Pelargonium graveolens*) in the old flower gardens. Recently, it's decided to take up throughout the broken concrete paths that border those flower beds. It's a pretty, flowering plant that falls within the geranium family. Its leaves are scented and heady, and are great for cooking with. They have a unique flavour and are often used to perfume sugars, ice creams, cakes, jams and syrups. Rhubarb and rose is an incredible combination and one I've played with many times in the past. But the flavour from the rose-scented geranium leaf is even more lovely.

SERVES 4

4 large rhubarb sticks, trimmed and cut into 8–10cm (3¼–4in) pieces

2 tablespoons golden caster sugar

2 tablespoons runny honey

8–10 rose geranium leaves

Heat the oven to 150°C/300°F/gas mark 3.

Arrange the rhubarb pieces in a single layer over a large shallow baking dish. Scatter over the sugar, trickle over the honey and 2 tablespoons of water and tear over the geranium leaves. Turn everything together.

Cover the dish tightly with a piece of foil and place in the oven for 20–35 minutes, or until the rhubarb is soft but not broken down. (timings will depend on how thick the chunks are). Remove from the oven and set aside to cool.

I like to serve the rhubarb and its rosy geranium syrup with vanilla custard, and perhaps a buttery shortbread biscuit or two.

quince & vanilla crème brûlée

There are patterns in the way we live – we repeat the same movements and motions every day, without even thinking about it. We open our eyes, stir our coffee, close the front door, say hello, eat some fruit, press space bar, press return. When do we ever crack a layer of burnt sugar with a spoon?

MAKES 4

2 quinces, peeled, quartered, cored and sliced thinly

juice of ½ lemon

75g (2½oz) sugar

50ml (2fl oz) whole milk

250ml (9fl oz) double cream

1 vanilla pod, split and seeds scraped, pod reserved

3 large egg yolks

4 heaped teaspoons caster sugar, for the topping

Place the quinces in a medium pan with about 200ml (7fl oz) of water, the lemon juice and 25g (1oz) of the sugar. Bring to a simmer, cover and cook for 15–30 minutes, or until the quinces are soft and thick.

Remove the quinces from the heat and divide them equally between four ramekins or small bowls. Smooth the quince level with the back of a spoon and place the ramekins or dishes in the fridge to chill.

Heat the oven to 120°C/235°F/gas mark 1. Pour the milk and cream into a medium pan. Add the vanilla seeds and the scraped pod to the pan. Place over a low heat, bring to a simmer, then turn off the heat. Allow to stand for 5 minutes for the flavours to infuse.

Combine the egg yolks and remaining sugar together in a large mixing bowl, but don't over mix. Remove and discard the vanilla pod from the pan with the milk and cream mixture, then pour the hot mixture over the eggs and whisk well.

Strain the vanilla custard through a sieve into a clean jug. Pour equal amounts of the custard gently over the quince in each ramekin or dish. If you pour it over the back of a spoon, it won't break up the fruit too much. Place the ramekins or dishes in a deep baking tray and pour in enough boiling water to come two-thirds of the way up the sides of each ramekin. Bake in the oven for about 20–30 minutes or until just set. The puddings should have a slight wobble to their middles. Remove from the oven and the baking tray, allow to cool, then refrigerate until needed.

To serve, scatter a heaped teaspoon of caster sugar over the top of the custard in each ramekin or dish. Flash the puddings under a hot grill or caramelize the sugar with a blow torch until golden and bubbling. Leave to cool for 15–20 minutes before serving.

a sloe gin

Sloes that have seen a frost or two are perfect for this kind of gin making. It's the cold kiss that helps break down their tough outer skin and free the sharp sloe juice from within. It seems, though, the frosts are becoming fewer and further between these days. It is possible, however, to replicate this frosty effect by popping the sloes in the freezer for a few hours before using.

MAKES ABOUT 3 X 750ML (26FL OZ) BOTTLES

500g (1lb 2oz) sloes

600ml (21fl oz) good-quality gin

300–450g (10½–1lb) golden granulated or caster sugar (the amount you use will depend upon how sweet you like your sloe gin)

Place the sloes, gin and sugar in a 2-litre (70fl oz) jar. Give it a shake to help dissolve the sugar and then simply leave it for about 6–8 weeks, if you can. A gentle shake of the jar every so often will ensure the sloes are doing what the gin is asking.

When you're ready to bottle your sloe gin, line a sieve with a clean muslin cloth and set it over a large jug. Pour the contents of the jar into the muslin to strain the liqueur, then pour the liqueur into clean, sealable bottles. Use as needed. It will keep for several years.

I once used the leftover gin-soaked sloe flesh in a batch of chocolate truffles, and they were, dare I say so myself, quite delicious.

index

Publishing Director and Editor: Sarah Lavelle
Designer: Miranda Harvey
Photographer: Andrew Montgomery
Copy Editor: Judy Barratt
Production: Vincent Smith and Stephen Lang

First published in 2018 by Quadrille, an imprint of Hardie Grant Publishing

Quadrille
52–54 Southwark Street
London SE1 1UN
quadrille.com

Text © Gill Meller 2018
Photography © Andrew Montgomery 2018
Design and layout © Quadrille Publishing Limited 2018

Photographs on p.127 and p.128 by Andrew Montgomery,
courtesy of *Delicious* magazine

Cataloguing in Publication Data: a catalogue record for this book
is available from the British Library.

ISBN: 978 1 78713 031 9

Printed in China

NOTES ON THE RECIPES

Unless otherwise specified, use:
Sea salt flakes, preferably Maldon
Medium free-range or organic eggs
Fresh herbs (all parsley is flat-leaf)
Medium vegetables
Whole-fat dairy products
Unwaxed lemons
Salted butter
Organic, free-range meat whenever you can,
and fish from sustainable sources

Oven temperatures are for a fan-assisted oven.
Use metric or imperial measurements, not a mixture of the two.

acknowledgements

Each year I become more aware of time and how quickly it seems to pass. I become more aware of what matters, which, in turn, makes me realise what doesn't.

In the end, the most important things we can do in life are to help each other, be kind and say thank you. Everything else is just paper in the wind.

Although *Time* has been a personal project, it wouldn't have happened without the support of my family, friends and the small team that works with me.

First and foremost, I'd like to thank my wife, Alice. Thank you for everything you do, and have done, to make the time we have the best it can be. Thank you to my daughters, Isla and Coco – each time I see you both I feel a sense of relief.

Andrew Montgomery's photographs have made *Time* the book I hoped it would be. His work is extraordinarily beautiful. Thank you for your resolve and your uncompromising eye.

Sarah Lavelle, thank you so much for seeing what I saw. The way you do things makes books better.

Thank you Miranda Harvey for turning a collection of words and pictures into something we can all hold, looks beautiful, and will always be here. You've done a really amazing thing.

Thank you to my editor Jude Barratt, for fixing it all up in the most unnoticeable way. I still don't know how you do that.

Thank you to my agent and sounding board, Antony Topping; and to everyone else at Greene and Heaton.

To my family and friends who let Andrew and me into the hearts of their homes. The pictures we took of your kitchens have given this book such depth, character and honesty. I'm so grateful to you all for sharing such a personal space. So, in no particular order, thank you Jessamy Upton, Tristan Connell, my Dad Barrie, Oliver & Kerry Goolden, Mew, Julian & Diana Temperley, Cameron Short & Janet Tristram, Hugh & Candida Dunford Wood, Tania Kovats & Alex Hartley, Sarah & Paul Appleby, Simon & Ines Ford, Pamela Dixon and Andrew and Malwina Tyrrell, and thanks to Hope Pointing for all her valuable help in the kitchen.

Thanks must also go out to Hugh Fearnley-Whittingstall and everyone I work with at River Cottage. Thanks to the fantastic teams at Quadrille Publishing and Hardie Grant – without them I wouldn't have made this book.

I'd like to say thank you to Karen Barnes and everyone else I've been working with at *Delicious* magazine. What a team!

I'd like to thank Ashley & Kate Wheeler, Will Livingstone, and Harry & Emily for the amazing ingredients they grow. Thank you to the wonderful Diana Henry and equally wonderful Nigella Lawson for your ongoing support. Thanks to Oliver Gladwin, Simon & Fiona Wheeler, Sarah Jarath, Rebecca Proctor, Blenheim Forge, Chloé Rosetta Bell, Lydia Johnson, Dan Prendergast, Peter Hitchin and Melanie Molesworth.

Lastly, thank you to my Mum, who I miss every day; and to my Dad, the man I look up to the most. Thank you to my brother Patrick and my sister Rose and to James, Jess, Beatrix, Benedict and Pearl. X